Unreal Engine 4 Game Development Quick Start Guide

Programming professional 3D games with Unreal Engine 4

Rachel Cordone

BIRMINGHAM - MUMBAI

Unreal Engine 4 Game Development Quick Start Guide

Commissioning Editor: Pavan Ramchandani
Acquisition Editor: Siddharth Mandal
Content Development Editor: Roshan Kumar
Technical Editor: Sushmeeta Jena
Copy Editor: Safis Editing
Project Coordinator: Namrata Swetta
Proofreader: Safis Editing
Indexer: Pratik Shirodkar
Graphics: Alishon Mendonsa
Production Coordinator: Nilesh Mohite

First published: May 2019

Production reference: 1270519

Published by Packt Publishing Ltd.
Livery Place
35 Livery Street
Birmingham
B3 2PB, UK.

ISBN 978-1-78995-068-7

www.packtpub.com

Mapt

Mapt is an online digital library that gives you full access to over 5,000 books and videos, as well as industry leading tools to help you plan your personal development and advance your career. For more information, please visit our website.

Why subscribe?

- Spend less time learning and more time coding with practical eBooks and Videos from over 4,000 industry professionals

- Improve your learning with Skill Plans built especially for you

- Get a free eBook or video every month

- Mapt is fully searchable

- Copy and paste, print, and bookmark content

Packt.com

Did you know that Packt offers eBook versions of every book published, with PDF and ePub files available? You can upgrade to the eBook version at www.packt.com and as a print book customer, you are entitled to a discount on the eBook copy. Get in touch with us at customercare@packtpub.com for more details.

At www.packt.com, you can also read a collection of free technical articles, sign up for a range of free newsletters, and receive exclusive discounts and offers on Packt books and eBooks.

Contributors

About the author

Rachel Cordone is a game designer and programmer who has been working with the Unreal Engine since the 1990's. She has worked with various game and simulation companies since 2003 on everything from PC, console, mobile, to VR and AR projects. For the past decade, Rachel has offered remote contract programming services to training software development companies including Northrop Grumman and Parsons Brinkerhoff. On the side, she makes video games through her company, Stubborn Horse Studios. She also wrote the book *Unreal Development Kit Game Programming with UnrealScript* for Packt.

I would like to thank all of the floppy-eared goats of the world, and my fiance for his support.

About the reviewer

Katax Emperore first encountered digital games when he got the *Fire Attack* series by Nintendo. One game stuck with him, a platform-based game called *Shadow of the Beast* by Psygnosis. He designs, develops, and teaches game design and programming. The Amiga platform created a high-quality gaming experience supported by an advanced architecture. It was a popular computer with real stereo sound, supported by advanced Direct Memory Access technology. He learned many aspects of programming, multitasking, DMA, interactive applications, I/O port mappings, graphic design, and 3D programming. When Microsoft introduced Windows 98, he learned programming, and 3D and graphic design, which led him to dedicate his education and career to the IT industry.

> *I am grateful to John Carmack, from id Software, for his efforts and great work on 3D graphic programming. What he invented back in 90's was the beginning of the wonderful genre of first-person shooter games. Also, I would like to thank Westwood Studios for introducing the Command and Conquer series to the gaming world. This game pioneered many aspects of modern real-time strategy games, which later powered many sub-genres in this area as well.*

Packt is searching for authors like you

If you're interested in becoming an author for Packt, please visit authors.packtpub.com and apply today. We have worked with thousands of developers and tech professionals, just like you, to help them share their insight with the global tech community. You can make a general application, apply for a specific hot topic that we are recruiting an author for, or submit your own idea.

Table of Contents

Preface

Unreal Engine 4 (UE4) can make developing your own games simple, even for those who have no prior programming experience. This book will get you up to speed with the major features of UE4 quickly, and leave you with the resources required to expand your knowledge through other tutorials and official documentation.

Each chapter builds and expands on a working game. It won't be anything fancy, but you'll be able to see how UE4's systems interact by means of a working example.

Who this book is for

This book is aimed at readers who already have some game development experience and would suit Unity users who would like to try UE4. It is assumed that the reader has knowledge of basic object-oriented programming topics such as variables, functions, and classes.

What this book covers

Chapter 1, *Introduction to Unreal Engine 4*, looks into how Unreal Engine can be downloaded and installed. We will get a head start on the project's development. We will also learn how to use plugins and marketplace items to expand on the editor's capabilities and further simplify our own project's development.

Chapter 2, *Programming Using Blueprints*, shows how to create custom Blueprint classes and use variables and functions within Blueprint classes. You will also gain an understanding of the differences between functions and events.

Chapter 3, *Adding C++ to a Blueprint Project*, covers creating and using classes in UE4. You will also learn to create custom Blueprint Events in C++.

Chapter 4, *Creating HUDs and Menus Using UMG*, teaches you how to create widgets and how to set them up as menus and HUDs. It also demonstrates some of the more advanced uses of widgets, such as adding widgets to other widgets.

Chapter 5, *Animation Blueprints*, introduces a lot of information about Animation Blueprints and how to use them to make a character more dynamic. You will also learn how to modify a blueprint by taking various factors into account when creating a character.

Chapter 6, *AI with Behavior Tree and Blackboard*, shows how to create some simple AI by making your own Pawn and Controller with some code to make them run around a NavMesh. You will also learn how to set up a Blackboard and how to use sequences, selectors, tasks, decorators, and services.

Chapter 7, *Multiplayer Games*, talks about multiplayer games and the different designs and thought processes that go into them. We will also get a clear idea of how to go about creating a multiplayer game without getting caught in some of the common pitfalls.

Chapter 8, *Optimization, Testing, and Packaging*, talks about optimization, testing, and packaging. You will also learn about debugging UE4 and packaging your game for distribution.

To get the most out of this book

Readers should have some previous programming experience, as this book includes explanations on how UE4 uses variables and functions with the Blueprint system.

Download the example code files

You can download the example code files for this book from your account at www.packt.com. If you purchased this book elsewhere, you can visit www.packt.com/support and register to have the files emailed directly to you.

You can download the code files by following these steps:

1. Log in or register at www.packt.com.
2. Select the **SUPPORT** tab.
3. Click on **Code Downloads & Errata**.
4. Enter the name of the book in the **Search** box and follow the onscreen instructions.

Once the file is downloaded, please make sure that you unzip or extract the folder using the latest version of:

- WinRAR/7-Zip for Windows
- Zipeg/iZip/UnRarX for Mac
- 7-Zip/PeaZip for Linux

The code bundle for the book is also hosted on GitHub at `https://github.com/PacktPublishing/Unreal-Engine-4-Game-Development-Quick-Start-Guide`. In case there's an update to the code, it will be updated on the existing GitHub repository.

We also have other code bundles from our rich catalog of books and videos available at `https://github.com/PacktPublishing/`. Check them out!

Download the color images

We also provide a PDF file that has color images of the screenshots/diagrams used in this book. You can download it here: `https://www.packtpub.com/sites/default/files/downloads/9781789950687_ColorImages.pdf`.

Conventions used

There are a number of text conventions used throughout this book.

`CodeInText`: Indicates code words in text, database table names, folder names, filenames, file extensions, pathnames, dummy URLs, user input, and Twitter handles. Here is an example: "In our `ThirdPersonCharacter` blueprint, this can be seen with the `CameraBoom` and `FollowCamera` components"

A block of code is set as follows:

```
if ( MyActorReference != null )
{
    // This is the Is Valid output.
}
else
{
    // This is the Is Not Valid output.
}
```

When we wish to draw your attention to a particular part of a code block, the relevant lines or items are set in bold:

```
if ( MyActorReference != null )
{
    // This is the Is Valid output.
}
else
{
    // This is the Is Not Valid output.
}
```

Bold: Indicates a new term, an important word, or words that you see onscreen. For example, words in menus or dialog boxes appear in the text like this. Here is an example: "Click on the **Input** subsection."

Warnings or important notes appear like this.

Tips and tricks appear like this.

Get in touch

Feedback from our readers is always welcome.

General feedback: If you have questions about any aspect of this book, mention the book title in the subject of your message and email us at customercare@packtpub.com.

Errata: Although we have taken every care to ensure the accuracy of our content, mistakes do happen. If you have found a mistake in this book, we would be grateful if you would report this to us. Please visit www.packt.com/submit-errata, selecting your book, clicking on the Errata Submission Form link, and entering the details.

Piracy: If you come across any illegal copies of our works in any form on the Internet, we would be grateful if you would provide us with the location address or website name. Please contact us at copyright@packt.com with a link to the material.

If you are interested in becoming an author: If there is a topic that you have expertise in and you are interested in either writing or contributing to a book, please visit authors.packtpub.com.

Reviews

Please leave a review. Once you have read and used this book, why not leave a review on the site that you purchased it from? Potential readers can then see and use your unbiased opinion to make purchase decisions, we at Packt can understand what you think about our products, and our authors can see your feedback on their book. Thank you!

For more information about Packt, please visit packt.com.

Introduction to Unreal Engine 4

Welcome to **Unreal Engine 4 (UE4)**! Unreal Engine can make developing your own games simple, even for those of you with no prior programming experience. But, it is important to familiarize yourself with some of the major systems to save yourself time and headaches down the line. This book will get you up to speed with the major features of UE4 quickly, and leave you with the resources required to expand on your knowledge through other tutorials and official documentation.

This book is intended for people with some previous programming experience. I won't go into detail about how variables and functions work, but I will explain how UE4 uses them with the Blueprint system. We will go into more detail about some systems that are specific to game programming or to the UE itself, such as UMG and multiplayer.

We will use examples to learn. Each chapter will build and expand on a working game. It won't be anything fancy, but you'll be able to see how UE4's systems interact by means of a working example.

In this chapter, we will cover the following topics:

- Downloading and installing the Unreal Engine
- Using Project Templates to save time developing basic functionality
- Explore the layout of the editor so we know where to find what we need in order to develop our game
- Examine the settings we can use to fully customize our game and the editor itself to save development time
- Adding plugins and marketplace items to further expand your development possibilities

So with that, let's get started!

Downloading the UE

Before we get into the engine itself, we need to download and install it as follows:

1. Search the internet for `Unreal Engine`, or head to this address at `https://www.unrealengine.com`.
2. Create a free account with Epic Games and log in to it.
3. In the top right of the Unreal Engine site, you will find a link to the download. Download the **Epic Games** launcher.
4. Once it's done downloading, go ahead and install it.
5. Once that's done, open it up. This will load the **Epic Games** launcher.
6. When the launcher opens, click the **Unreal Engine** button on the left-hand side:

7. Here, you will have four useful tabs at the top:

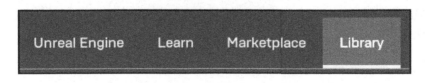

Here is a description of the items you can see in the preceding screenshot:

- **Unreal Engine**: In addition to featured content, there are links to **AnswerHub** (like Stack Overflow, but UE4-specific), **Forums**, and a **Wiki**, with tutorials and engine documentation. There are also links to the **Roadmap** and **Blog** to see current and upcoming developments involving the engine.
- **Learn**: This is a more detailed tab for developers to find tutorials and documentation. This tab also includes demos and other samples. This is a great place to find inspiration for features that might otherwise not have been on your mind.
- **Marketplace**: This is the UE asset store. Art, code, animation, and plugins can all be found here. There is a free section to get you started, and frequent sales, so keep an eye on it!
- **Library**: This tab keeps track of your currently installed engine versions, your projects, and your marketplace purchases for easy installation.

8. This **Library** tab is where we will begin. You can choose to install any engine version all the way back to 4.0.2, but, for the purpose of this book, we will be using the latest version, which is 4.22.1 at the time of writing.
9. To start the installation, press the plus sign next to **Engine Versions** and select **4.22.1** with the drop-down arrow, and then press **Install**:

Once that's done, the **Install** button should change to **Launch**, for example. For each project's initial setup, you'll press this button to launch whichever engine version you want the project to use. After that, the project will appear in your **My Projects** list and you can launch them that way. You can also right-click on a project in the **My Projects** list to create a shortcut for it. That way, you won't even need to run the **Epic Games** launcher to dive right back into your project.

For now, hit the **Launch** button on 4.22.1. The project browser will appear, as follows:

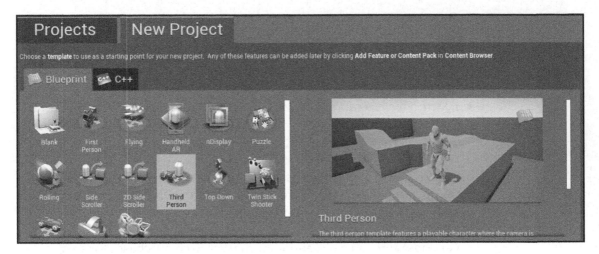

All of your existing projects will show in the **Projects** tab along with their engine version. Projects cannot be opened with a previous version of the engine, but it's usually fine to open a project with a later engine version.

You will just need to make sure any plugins your project uses will be compatible with the newer engine version.

Using project templates

In the **New Project** tab, you will find templates for various project types. These templates will give you a great head start, so you won't need to reinvent code that is common to specific game types. The templates are as follows:

- **Blank**: Only use this option if none of the following templates fit your project's genre. Usually, one of the other templates will cover what you need to get started, and everything about the template can be customized or deleted. But if your game project doesn't fall under anything else, you can use this option to create your entire game from scratch.
- **First Person**: This is the standard shooter template. It includes a first person arm mesh and a weapon that fires projectiles.
- **Flying**: This is a third-person view of a spaceship that can be flown around.
- **Handheld AR**: This includes everything you need to get started with augmented reality on a phone. Make sure your device supports ARKit for iOS devices, or ARCore for Android!

- **nDisplay**: This option is used for multimonitor/cave display setups. It is rarely used, but is an incredibly useful template when you need it.
- **Puzzle**: Most people associate the UE with top-of-the-line graphics, but even simple puzzle games can benefit from the workflow that Blueprints present.
- **Rolling**: Ball-based games will find their home here. All of these templates have keyboard, gamepad, and touch inputs already set up as appropriate. Here, the ball can be controlled with any of the three options.
- **Side Scroller / 2D Side Scroller**: This is a standard Metroidvania camera setup. Which of these two you use depends on whether your art assets will be 2D or 3D.
- **Third Person**: This is a free rotating camera with a keyboard-controlled player, common for platformers and action games.
- **Top Down**: This can be easily confused with the **Third Person** template, but this one has a fixed camera with a Diablo style click-to-move player.
- **Twin Stick Shooter**: This is the **Top Down** shooter template. Don't let the icon fool you; this template is just as suitable for a Hotline Miami style human player as it is for a bullet-hell spaceship one.
- **Vehicle**: This is the racing template. Another great feature of these templates is the ability to combine them. For instance, if you wanted to make a GTA style game where you could run around or drive cars, you could choose the **Third Person** template, and once you're in the Unreal editor, you could add the **Vehicle** template to your project as well.
- **Virtual Reality**: This includes hand models, teleportation, and grabbable objects.
- **Vehicle Advanced**: If your project needs more realistic vehicles than the simple physics of the vehicle template, this would be your choice.

Most of these templates can be used in both Blueprint and C++ projects (**augmented reality (AR)** and **virtual reality (VR)** templates are Blueprint only). Unless your goal is to solely use Blueprints or C++, don't worry too much about which project type to use. C++ can be added to Blueprint projects and vice versa.

One major exception to this is if you need to alter any of the engine code itself, or if you need dedicated servers for your game. Using the UE through the launcher with the official engine versions allows us to extend from the engine and its classes, but it doesn't let us modify the engine code directly. If you do need to do this, you will need to download and compile the engine yourself, which is fairly simple but outside the scope of this quick start guide. Most of the time, you can create and deploy your entire game without needing to touch the engine code.

Initial project setup

For this book, we will be using a Blueprint project with the **Third Person** template, so select that.

Next, we need to choose from a few other options. These can also be changed later, so don't worry about choosing incorrectly. Here are the selections we need to make:

- **Desktop / Console** or **Mobile**: For this book, we will be using **Desktop / Console** as our target hardware.
- **Maximum Quality** or **Scalable**: We will use **Maximum Quality** here. Graphics settings can be changed once the project is created, and we will discuss some of those options later in this chapter.
- **With** or **Without Starter Content**: Most of the time, you'll want to include the starter content for quick prototyping. These assets can always be deleted from your project once they're no longer needed, but they are a great help when creating test levels:

Now, give your project a name and location and click **Create Project**. I will be naming the project AwesomeGame, because we're awesome and your game will be awesome:

Now, we have to wait while the project is being created. This will take a while, and it might seem like it gets stuck at 90-something percent, but give it time and eventually, we'll get our first look at the editor!

The Unreal editor

Once the editor finishes loading, we will get our first look at it. This is what we will see:

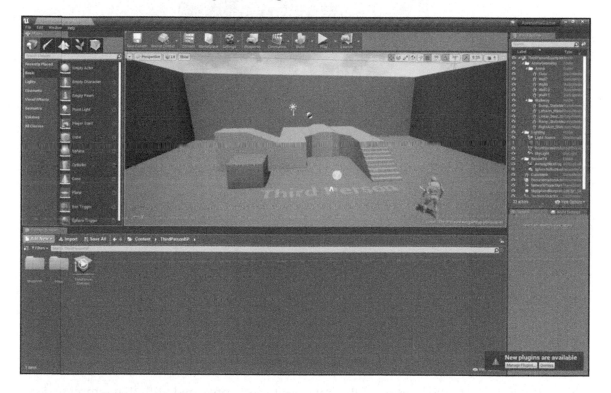

The editor's layout will quickly be decipherable to anyone who has used Unity or another game engine before, but there's always the fear of clicking something and having everything go wonky, so let's take it panel by panel. We'll start at the bottom left with the **Content Browser**.

The Content Browser

This is where all of our game's content will appear, from code to static meshes, materials, sounds, and animations. If we press the arrow button in the top-left corner above the folders, we can see a complete folder view for the content in our project, as shown in the following screenshot:

To get a quick overview of the template you're using, you can press the play icon on the **ThirdPerson Overview** asset (the ThirdPersonBP folder in our case) as shown in the following screenshot:

This will point you to the location of the important assets provided with that template. For the ThirdPerson template, the two assets we'll be digging into the most are the ThirdPersonCharacter and ThirdPersonGameMode under ThirdPersonBP\Blueprints.

At the end of the overview, a **Tutorials** tab will pop up with links to tutorials for everything from C++ to animation and landscapes. You can also find a link to this tab under **Help | Tutorials**.

Back to the **Content Browser**, if you look at the top, you'll see the **Add New** button. This lets you create a new asset of any type, including Blueprints, behavior trees for AI, and sound cues. At the top of this list, you'll see **Add Feature or Content Pack**, which is what I was describing earlier in this chapter in the *Using project templates* section. If you require **Vehicle** template functionality in your `ThirdPerson` project, for example, this is where you would add it.

The Viewport

Next in our tour of the Unreal editor is the Viewport. This displays our currently loaded level and can be configured to make navigation easier. There are two ways to move the camera around in the Viewport:

- **Mouse and WASD**: Holding the right mouse button down will let you rotate the camera, while using the *WASD* keys will move the camera forward/backward and left/right. Anyone with experience in Unity will be used to this camera movement.
- **Mouse only**: It is also possible to navigate using only the mouse, which people with experience in previous Unreal editors will be familiar with. Holding the left mouse button will let you move the camera along the horizontal plane along with looking left/right. Holding the right mouse button will keep the camera in place while letting you look around. Holding both the left and right mouse buttons will let you move the camera up/down and left/right at the same time while keeping the rotation the same. Combining these three mouse button combinations will let you navigate a level without needing to use the keyboard.

 Pressing *F11* will let you toggle fullscreen on the Viewport.

Viewport options

On the upper left of the Viewport are a few drop-down menus that let us customize and configure the Viewport. Starting from the left with the drop-down arrow, a few of the important options are as follows:

- **Realtime**: This toggles real-time rendering of any animated elements of the level. You can see it with the spinning green **DocumentationActor**, but this also applies to any animated materials and particle effects. With this off, elements will only update while you are moving the camera.
- **Show Stats / Show FPS**: This toggles **frames per second** (FPS) and stats that show information such as poly counts, rendering times in milliseconds, and memory usage. A full list of stat options can be found in the **Stat** submenu a bit further down the menu.
- **Game View**: This toggles any editor-only icons and assets so you can see what the level will look like in game. Pressing G also toggles this, so if you've accidentally hidden the editor icons, it was probably this way.
- **Bookmarks**: This allows you to set bookmarks for camera locations so you can use keyboard numbers to teleport there. This option is incredibly useful and often overlooked, so getting into the habit of using these early can save you a lot of time navigating your levels. These are level-specific, making them even more useful, but don't forget to save your level if you change these; otherwise, you will lose them.
- **Layouts**: This lets you choose from a variety of Viewport layouts with up to four views. If, for some reason, you need even more Viewports, at the top of the editor, press **Window | Viewports** and select one of the other Viewports (**Viewport 1** is the existing one). Each of these can also be configured with up to four panes.
- **Advanced Settings**: This lets you further customize the Viewports by inverting the mouse, combining the translate/rotate widgets, and adjusting highlight intensity, among other things. Don't worry about messing things up here; you can always press the **Reset to Defaults** button in the top-right corner.

Next to the drop-down arrow at the top of the Viewport is **Perspective**. This is the setting for the Viewport type. By default, it shows a 3D perspective, but this can be configured to show a 2D wireframe view from the top or left, and so on.

Navigation while in a 2D perspective is a bit different than the 3D view. Holding the right mouse button lets you move around, and the mouse wheel lets you zoom in and out.

While in a 2D view, holding the left mouse button lets you drag a selection box. Another useful tool is holding the middle mouse button to use the measuring tool. This is useful for programmers when we're trying to figure out how far enemies should be able to see, for example.

Next in the Viewport options is the Viewport's visual style, which defaults to **Lit**. You can choose **Unlit** and **Wireframe** for example, but this also offers a lot of optimization views, such as **Shader Complexity** and **Collision** views. Most of these are more useful for artists.

The final dropdown in the upper-left corner is the **Show** list. This can be used to hide things that might be in your way, such as fog, or to show extra options, such as a collision. This includes a few advanced options, such as showing bones for skeletal meshes. This menu also includes a **Default** so that you can reset anything you've changed here.

Grid and snap settings

In the upper-right part of the Viewport are the settings for the translation tool, grid, snap, and camera:

- The first three buttons (labelled **1** previously) allow us to switch between translation, rotation, and scaling for world objects (although it's easier and quicker to use *W*, *E*, and *R* on the keyboard for this).
- Next is the global/local toggle (**2**). This changes the way the translation, rotation, and scaling work to be world oriented or dependent on the selected object's rotation.
- The next setting is the grid snap (**3**). The first button of these three (with a curve and three arrows) lets you toggle surface snapping, which will automatically place objects on the floor when moving them around, with an option to automatically rotate them to align with the floor's rotation.

 The Unreal editor bases its unit system on centimeters. Although this is all relative and you can choose any reference scale you want, the default character you control is built around 1 unreal *unit* = *1* centimeter.

- The next button (section **3**, second button), which is orange with a grid, toggles grid snapping completely. If you need to precisely align an object, turning grid snapping off will help with that.

- The final button in the grid snap section (section **3**, third button) lets you choose the grid snap distance. Lower values will let you adjust objects more finely.
- After the grid snap, we have the rotation snap (**4**) and scale snap (**5**) sections. They operate the same as the grid snap, and the scale snap has an additional option to preserve the ratio between the axes while scaling.
- The last option in the upper right of the Viewport controls the camera speed (**6**), with a scalar for more control over the range of speed.

The toolbar

Above the Viewport is the toolbar, as shown in the following screenshot:

This gives access to some of the more commonly used features of the editor:

- **Save Current**: This saves the current level. Save on a frequent basis. By default, the editor has autosave turned on, but it's set to 10 minutes, and that can be a lot of work when you're in the zone.
- **Source Control**: This hooks your content to subversion, perforce, or Git content control. If your team uses one of these, this will save a lot of time over having to do this outside of the editor.
- **Content**: This opens the **Content Browser** if you have that tab closed.
- **Marketplace**: Pressing this may seem like it does nothing, but it opens the **Marketplace** in the **Epic Games** launcher. You'll need to switch over to that program to see it, as it doesn't automatically pop back up.
- **Settings**: This provides access to some settings menus we'll be talking about in a bit, along with a number of selection, quality level, and snap settings for the Viewport.
- **Blueprints**: This lets you create and find Blueprint classes, but this is easier done in the **Content Browser**. This is also where you access the level-specific Blueprint.
- **Cinematics**: This is beyond the scope of this guide, but here is where you would get started with creating cinematics at your level.

- **Build**: Here is where you set the rebuild options for the level, and where you rebuild geometry, lighting, and pathing in the level. For programmers, most of this is not our focus, but you will want to rebuild pathing when working with AI, and doing a complete rebuild by simply pressing the **Build** button in the toolbar will get rid of the red **LIGHTING NEEDS TO BE REBUILT** notification in the Viewport and in game. To make things quicker, keep the **Lighting Quality** at **Preview** until you're ready to do non-test builds.

- **Play**: This lets you play the current level without having to build the entire project. By default, this uses the current Viewport, but exiting from this with *Esc* doesn't reset the camera, so I usually set this to **New Editor Window**. For multiplayer testing, you can also set the number of players, which will open a separate window for each one. If you have compiled the engine yourself and set up dedicated server functionality, you can enable that here as well. At the bottom is a link to **Advanced Settings**, such as mouse control, Viewport sizes, and server options.

- **Launch**: If you are developing for mobile or browser, you can launch to those devices from here.

World Outliner

The **World Outliner** tab on the right of the editor window contains a list of all of the objects in the current level, as shown in the following screenshot:

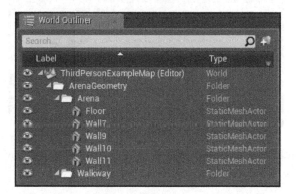

You can group them into folders, right-click to create a new folder, and click the eye icon on the left to hide individual objects or an entire folder at once. Selecting one or more objects here will display their properties in the **Details** panel (discussed in the next subsection). The right column will also have links to directly open the Blueprint associated with an object if it has one (such as the ThirdPersonCharacter for our project).

You can double-click on an item here to zoom the camera to that object. If you have an object selected, clicking it again will allow you to rename it to make organization easier.

This panel also has a **Search...** bar, which makes finding objects easier, especially combined with the renaming feature.

Right-clicking on an object in this panel provides more options for that object, including visibility, selecting matching objects, and attachment options. This same menu appears when you right-click on an object in the Viewport.

Details and World Settings

When an object is selected in a Viewport or in the **World Outliner** panel, its properties appear in the following screenshot:

Here, we can adjust each individual object in the level's properties. Most commonly, we can perform the following actions:

- Manually set `Location/Rotation/Scale` if we need precise values
- Set or find materials, meshes, and so on that it uses in the **Content Browser** (click the magnifying glass icon to go to that asset in the **Content Browser**)
- Adjust physics and lighting properties for that object (if it does not need to cast shadows for instance)

- Toggle visibility for the object so it appears in the editor but not in game (under the *Rendering* section of its properties)
- Adjust any custom properties we've added to our own objects (discussed in `Chapter 2`, *Programming Using Blueprints*)

Keep in mind that some of these properties are more easily changed without needing to do it here. For instance, for the material property of a static mesh, you can simply drag the material from the content browser on top of the object in the Viewport. You don't need to use the arrow button in the object's properties unless the object has multiple materials and you're having difficulty while setting up the right one.

World settings

Most of these properties aren't used too often, but there are a few here that interest us:

- **Enable World Composition**: For open world style games, this option would need to be enabled. Epic Games has good resources for creating this type of world. Searching for `UE4 World Composition` will provide you with plenty of tutorials for that.
- **KillZ**: This is the height at which actors get destroyed. If you're creating a level with a lot of height and your character keeps disappearing when you drop down, check this value to make sure it's low enough. It will appear as a red line in any of the side/front Viewports.
- **GameMode Override**: Instead of using the default `GameMode` class (which we will discuss with other **Project Settings** shortly), each level can override that with a specific `GameMode` class. For example, if you were making a third-person game, but one level was a car race, you could use this to set specific rules and character/HUD classes for this level, instead of needing to integrate both types of gameplay into one `GameMode` class. Once a `GameMode` override is set, each individual class default can be edited in the **Selected GameMode** dropdown beneath it.
- **Override World Gravity**: As with `GameMode`, instead of using the **Project Settings** value for gravity, each level can have its own.

Next, we will take a look at how to customize the editor itself with editor preferences to make our workflow easier.

Editor preferences

Back in the main editor window, if you go to **Edit | Editor Preferences** (near the bottom), you will see options to customize a lot of things pertaining to the editor. Let's go over some that are used more often:

- In the **Appearance** section, you can change the color of the grid and selected items, set colorblind options for the editor, and change the font size and color for the log.
- The **Keyboard Shortcuts** section has a complete list of the keyboard shortcuts the editor uses in its various windows and modes, and they are all completely customizable. Spend some time familiarizing yourself with them, as they will save you a lot of time when working on the editor.

- Next is the **Loading & Saving** section. Earlier, we talked about the autosave feature, and here is where you can change how it operates. By default, it is set to 10 minutes, but you can change that time here in the **Auto Save** section. You can also change what happens when you start up the editor as far as which level is loaded, and if it should restore any asset tabs you had open when you last shut down, which is pretty useful if you're working in a lot of different classes at a time and don't want to lose your place.

- Another section that you will want to take a look at is the **Play** section under **Level Editor**. Here, we can customize the **Play** in editor settings as well as the new window settings, changing the window size and the mouse/keyboard control scheme.

- You might not want to change most of these settings right away, but don't be scared to try them out. All of the sections here have a **Reset to Defaults** button if you need to revert your changes. You should definitely come back to these settings once you've had some experience with the editor and know more about what changes can improve your workflow.

Project settings

Next, we'll discuss the project settings under **Edit | Project Settings**:

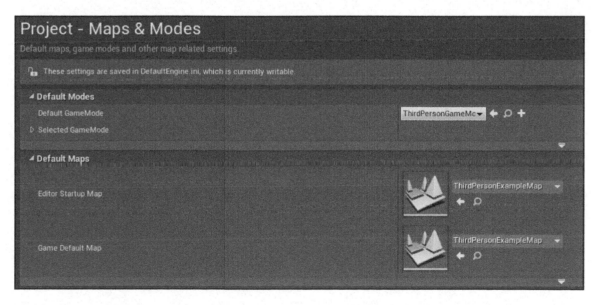

The first section we'll talk about is **Description**. Here is where you will set your project/company name, any copyright and licensing notices, and window settings for the game (resizeable, borderless window, and so on). You can also manually set your project thumbnail here, which will show up in the **Epic Games** launcher in your project library.

Next up is **Maps & Modes**. Here, you can change the default GameMode class for your game (which can be overridden per level as previously discussed). You can also set which level is loaded when the editor starts up and which level is loaded when the actual game starts up (usually a title screen level).

There are also options for split-screen multiplayer if your game uses that.

The last option here is the GameInstance class, which can store data across level loads.

The next section is **Movies**, which allows you to set any startup movies, such as company logos, and lets you set whether or not these are skippable. And please, on behalf of gamers everywhere, make these skippable.

The next section is **Packaging**. Here is where you set your project to a development or shipping build and set options such as whether or not to do a full rebuild each time you run one. You can also set the Blueprint nativization method if desired, which converts them to C++ during the build process and will be discussed more in Chapter 8, *Optimization, Testing, and Packaging*.

After that comes **Supported Hardware**, which is self-explanatory, and then **Target Hardware**. When we were first setting up our project, we set it to **Desktop / Console** and **Maximum Quality**. If you needed to change it, here is where that is done.

One last section you'll want to explore on your own is the **Engine** section. A lot of the defaults are set here for things such as AI movement, animation compression, and audio classes.

Further down in the **Engine** section are the physics defaults, where you can set things such as gravity (which, as discussed, can be overridden per level), terminal velocity, and friction settings.

The last part of the engine settings I want to talk about is rendering. Here is where the major components of the graphics will be adjusted, such as ambient occlusion and motion blur. Depending on the scope of your project, some of these will not be needed, and they can be individually disabled here to increase your game's performance and fit your game's art style.

Input settings

The input settings are part of the **Engine** section, but I want to discuss it separately from the other editor preferences. This section defines the keyboard, mouse, and gamepad inputs that our game will use, and will come into play in Chapter 2, *Programming Using Blueprints*. Let's take a look at the inputs that have been provided for our third-person project:

When you create your project, these inputs will automatically be created based on the template you use, but you will naturally want to add more depending on your gameplay. For instance, to add a Use key, you would press the plus sign next to **Action Mappings**, then change the name from NewActionMapping_0 to Use, and then select a keyboard key for it to use (*E* is common). Now, when you are creating or modifying your character class, you will be able to use this as an input event (discussed more in Chapter 2, *Programming Using Blueprints*).

Axis Mappings have an additional setting for scale, since they include gamepad thumbsticks that don't have a strict on/off state. If you look at **MoveForward** for example, you can see that the backward key (*S*) also calls the same input event; it just gives it a negative value so the character will move in the opposite direction.

Now that we've customized the editor with our preferences, let's look at how to further expand the engine's capabilities by using plugins.

Installing and using plugins

Plugins are packages of code that extend the functionality of the editor in a variety of ways. They can be used for importing file formats the UE is unfamiliar with by default, and add entirely new functionality, such as analytics.

Plugins can be found by going to **Edit** | **Plugins.** Once open, we can see a list of available plugins divided into categories:

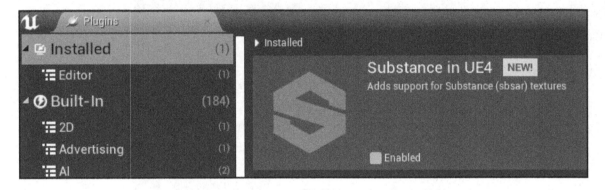

A lot of plugins are built into the engine and can be enabled or disabled as needed. Speaking of which, if you have Steam VR installed, you may have noticed that it started up automatically when the project launched. Since we're not going to be using any VR functionality in this book, let's disable that plugin now so Steam VR doesn't load every time we start up the editor:

1. To disable it, go to the **Plugins** browser.
2. Scroll all the way down on the left side and click on the **Virtual Reality** category.
3. On the right side, scroll down to Steam VR and uncheck it.
4. The editor will let you know that you need to restart for the setting to take effect, so click on the **Restart Now** button to do that.
5. Steam VR will not close on its own once you've done this though, so you will need to close that separately.

Plugins can also be downloaded and installed from third parties. One of the most useful ones, if you're making a multiplayer game, is the Advanced Sessions plugin by Joshua Statzer. This can be used to make it easier to set up multiplayer server browsers on Steam, for example. Download links can be found on the **Epic** forums by searching for UE4 Advanced Sessions. Once downloaded, you would need to create a Plugins folder in your project as follows:

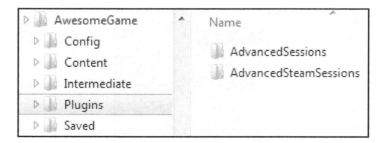

After creating the folder, you would place the Plugins folder inside (make sure the editor is shut down), and then start the editor back up, to have the plugin loaded. Most external plugins will provide documentation or example maps that have the relevant Blueprint classes and explanations on how to use them.

Adding marketplace items to your project

The final thing I want to discuss in this chapter is using marketplace items. The marketplace includes a lot of great assets you can use to speed up your prototype and development process. Why reinvent the wheel if you can save time and money? In addition to 3D models and materials, the marketplace is a good place to find Blueprint assets that give you a launching point for functionality in your game by providing things such as inventory systems or role playing game stat elements.

For this project, we will be downloading and installing one of the free packs provided by Epic, the **Animation Starter Pack**. It has weapon-oriented animations that we will be using in Chapter 5, *Animation Blueprints*, as we get into that topic. Let's follow these steps to download the pack:

1. Head back to the **Epic Games** launcher and search the marketplace for the **Animation Starter Pack**:

2. Add it to your cart and go through the checkout process, and the pack will appear in your **Library** tab in the **Vault** section underneath the **My Projects** section:

3. Click **Add To Project**, then select our `AwesomeGame` project. Once it's finished, you'll be able to see the folder in the **Content Browser**:

And that's it! Take a minute to browse the marketplace, since Epic has provided a lot of free content to start with, and some of the other content available there will save you a lot of development time and headaches.

Summary

In this chapter, we've downloaded and installed the Unreal Engine, and we've taken a look at the templates we can use to get a headstart on our project's development. We've broken down the editor panel by panel to get familiar with how everything is organized, and customized it using the editor preferences. Finally, we've seen how to use plugins and marketplace items to expand on the editor's capabilities and further simplify our own project's development.

As with any complex piece of software, the UE has a lot of systems that you will need to be familiar with in order to make full use of it. In the upcoming chapters, we will be going through most of the major ones, so you will be able to get a well-rounded crash course and know where to go to find any additional information you need.

First, we will be discussing Blueprints, a great alternative to traditional programming. It is easily possible to create entire games using Blueprints alone, without ever having to touch a line of code.

Having said that, we will also have a quick lesson on adding C++ to a Blueprint project to extend our Blueprint functionality.

We will also cover other major systems, such as using UMG to create menus and HUDs, animation Blueprints to control our character, and using replication to create multiplayer games.

Finally, we will talk about the final steps of a project, covering optimization, testing, and deployment.

Let's get started!

Programming Using Blueprints

2

Now, we have the Unreal engine installed and you have familiarized yourself with its layout. We've set up our project, looked at how to customize it, and we have added extra content with the Animation Starter Pack. Now, it's time to learn about Blueprints.

Blueprints are a powerful alternative to traditional C++ programming. As I said in the previous chapter, it is possible to create an entire game using only Blueprints. In this chapter, we will start laying the foundation for our Awesome Game using Blueprints, and, in later chapters, we will expand on this game so we can learn how to use other Unreal Engine 4 systems.

The following points will be covered in this chapter:

- Creating custom Blueprint classes and extending from Epic's base classes
- Using variables and functions within Blueprint classes
- Adding Components to a Blueprint class
- The difference between functions and events

Let's take our first look at a Blueprint window and start breaking it down.

The Blueprint window

To start working with Blueprints, we first need to go over the layout of a **Blueprint** window. In the **Content Browser**, go to `ThirdPersonBP\Blueprints` and double-click on `ThirdPersonCharacter`. The window that pops up should look like this:

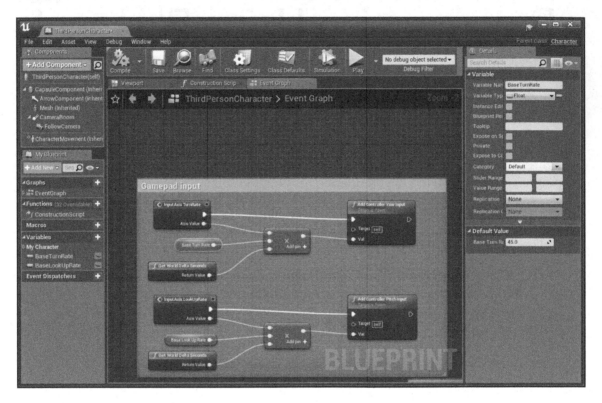

There's a lot going on here, so let's break it down tab by tab.

In the main window, we'll see our actual code. For our `ThirdPersonCharacter` class, we see the use of variables, operators, pure functions, and calls to other functions. We also see some tabs at the top of this—**Viewport**, **Construction Script**, and **Event Graph**. Every function we open will appear as a tab here. These will be discussed in the **Graphs** and **Viewport** sections later in this chapter.

In the bottom-left corner of the window, we will see the **My Blueprint** tab, which holds all of the **Graphs**, **Functions**, **Macros**, **Variables**, and **Event Dispatchers** for this class:

Let's break this tab down so we can learn how to use each individual part. While doing so, we will also learn about other parts of the **Blueprint** window.

Variables

First up, are variables. Since we assume you have some previous programming experience, we won't be explaining the difference between an int and a float, but, at the same time, switching from traditional text to UE4's node-based visual programming can sometimes leave you a bit frustrated when trying to do basic things. Hopefully, I will be able to help with that part.

Pressing the plus sign on the right-hand side of the **Variables** section will create a new variable. By default, this will be a Boolean (red), or it will be the same type as the previously modified one if you've already created one:

If you click on a selected variable again, you can rename it. To the right of the variable is a shortcut for setting this variable to public or protected (it defaults to protected).

When a variable is selected, you will also see a **Details** panel on the far right-hand side of the **Blueprint** window:

Here, we will be able to set some properties for our variable:

- **Variable Name**: This field is another way we can set the name our variable uses. Variable names can include spaces.
- **Variable Type**: This covers everything from floats to vectors, enums, structs and actor references. Any custom Blueprint classes that we've created will be selectable as well. The popup also has a search bar to make it easier to find the class you're looking for. If you're selecting an object, hovering over it will give you the option of selecting between an actual object reference or just a class reference if you need that instead (for example, a variable that determines what type of weapon a player will spawn with).

- **Instance Editable**: This sets whether the variable is public or protected.
- **Blueprint Read Only**: This stipulates whether you can set this variable or only read from it (effectively, a const variable).
- **Tooltip**: This will show a bit of text when you hover over the variable in the **Variables** section of the **My Blueprint** tab. This is particularly helpful when the **Variable Name** isn't self-explanatory.
- **Expose on Spawn**: This allows this variable to be initialized when the object is created. It is equivalent to initializing variables in the constructor in C++.
- **Private**: Although **Private** and **Instance Editable** can both be checked at the same time, **Private** takes precedence. If it is checked, child Blueprints will not be able to access this variable even if **Instance Editable** is checked.
- **Expose to Cinematics**: This allows the variable to be changed within level sequences so that it can be changed during cutscenes or cinematics.
- **Category**: This is incredibly useful for organizing your Blueprint classes. As your game's development progresses, some classes can have a lot of variables. This will let you organize them within the **Variables** section of the **My Blueprint** tab. Typing a new name into this box will create a new category.
- **Slider Range**: If you click and hold the left mouse button in the variable's value box (where it says 45.0 in the preceding pic), you can adjust the value by moving the mouse left and right. Setting the **Slider Range** allows you to limit the range of this variable when adjusted this way. This will only apply to certain variable types.
- **Value Range**: This sets the clamp values for the default value of this variable. This overrides the **Slider Range** if those values are outside the **Value Range**. Note that this only affects the default value of this variable. It can still be set to values outside this range in code. If you need the value clamped at all times, the best way to do it would be to make the variable **Private** and use custom **Set/Get** functions. (Creating functions is discussed after this **Variable** section).
- **Replication**: In multiplayer games, this is used to set the replication property of the variable. Using variable replication will be discussed in *Chapter 7, Multiplayer Games*.

There are a few other uncommon properties beneath the down arrow in this variable section for controlling things, such as config and transient variables. More information about those can be found in the UE4 documentation online: https://docs.unrealengine.com/en-us/Engine/Blueprints/UserGuide/Variables.

One final property that can be changed for variables is turning them into an array, set, or dictionary. This can be done by clicking on the icon to the right of the **Variable Type**:

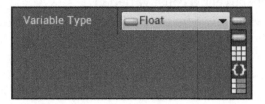

Now that we know how to create our own variables and modify their properties, let's take a look at how they are used in Blueprint code.

Using variables in the Blueprint window

If you click and drag one of the variables from the **My Blueprint** tab on the left-hand side of the Blueprint window into the main Blueprint area and let go of the left mouse button, the editor will give you an option to create either a **Get** or a **Set** for that variable:

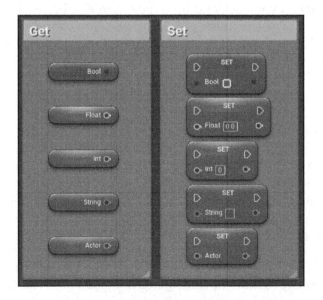

To make a connection from any node in a **Blueprint** window, just click and hold on any input pin (left side) or output pin (right side) and drag a connection to where you need it.

In certain cases, it is possible to drag connections between different variable types, such as **Float | String** or **Int | Bool**. If a conversion is available, it will automatically create the conversion node between the connecting points.

There is no limit to the number of connections *from* a variable node to other nodes, but, in some cases, variable inputs are limited to one connection. Some functions, such as *Set Actor Hidden In Game*, allow you to connect more than one variable to its input, however, so check whether this is the case to save time and maintain cleaner Blueprint code.

For Set nodes, you can connect a Get node's output or the output of some other operation into the set's input, or leave the input unconnected and hard code a value. (For example, the Set Float and Set Int nodes in the preceding screenshot will set the value to zero if no input is connected.) In most cases, you will want to connect a variable, but in a few cases, there will be a good reason to leave it unconnected:

- **String variables**: Leaving the Set input unconnected will clear the current value, making it an empty string.
- **Actor references**: Leaving the Set input unconnected will null the variable.

Note that Set nodes for an array *must* have an input connection. In order to clear an array, use a Get node, and create a Clear node to connect it to.

If you drag an output pin into an empty area and let go, the editor will offer up a list of possible operations and functions that can use it (including the Clear node for arrays mentioned previously). Most of the variable type-specific functions, such as NOT for Booleans, or math operations for ints and floats, can be found under the Math and Utility sections of this pop-up tab:

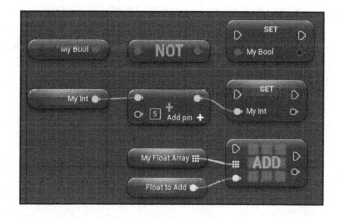

The popup will also have a search bar to make finding functions and operations easier. In some cases, these nodes can be found in multiple ways (typing `if` will bring up the branch node for Bools, for instance):

Also included in this list are any functions that take that variable type. For Bools, typing in **Set Actor Hidden** will bring up that function, for example:

By default, **Context Sensitive** is checked in this popup. This will limit the search to functions that can use that variable type and functions that are specific to the `Blueprint` class that you are using. If you are accessing a variable from another class, functions specific to that class will show. If you need to use a function and you know it exists, but it is not showing up in this list, unchecking this box will help you find it. Take care when doing this, however. If a function isn't showing up in the **Context Sensitive** list, you may be trying to use it incorrectly.

Another shortcut to use when working with variables is **Promote to Variable**. In the **Set Actor Hidden In Game** function call previously, if we didn't already have a Bool to connect to it, we could simply right-click the **New Hidden** input node and select **Promote To Variable**. This will automatically create and connect a new **Bool** to that input.

One final option when working with variables on the input pin is the Select functionality, which acts as a ternary operator (Condition ? UseIfTrue : UseIfFalse) but can have more than two outputs (acting more as a switch statement):

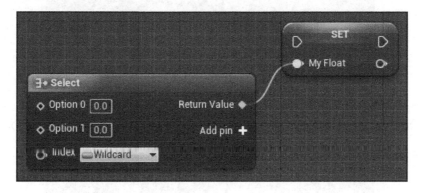

Dragging a connection off an input and typing Select will bring up this node as an option.

For the **Index** input, we can attach an int, byte, Bool, or any type of enum. Attaching a Bool will limit the input to two options for true or false. An enum will provide an input for every option in that enumerator. For ints and bytes, the options will start at 0 and go as high as you need (press the **Add Pin** button until you have the amount that you need).

Working With Object/Actor References

As with traditional programming, we need to avoid errors in our code that can occur from trying to access null variables. In Blueprints, there are a few ways in which we can make sure a variable is valid before using it:

- Depending on the context, we may just need true or false (uncommon, but may be required in an if statement before a function call, for example).
- The second method uses an IsValid function call with two outputs. Both of these can be found by typing valid in the search box.

- The third method, which I prefer, is to use a Validated Get, which can be created by right-clicking on a normal Get node and clicking on **Convert to Validated Get**. This is essentially the same as the second method, but keeps the code cleaner:

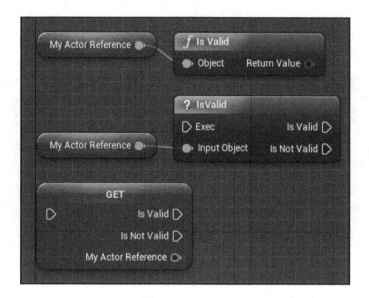

Using a validated GET is the same as this snippet of code:

```
if ( MyActorReference != null )
{
 // This is the Is Valid output.
}
else
{
 // This is the Is Not Valid output.
 }
```

The **Is Valid** output ensures that the `MyActorReference` variable isn't null, and you won't get any errors trying to access its variables and functions:

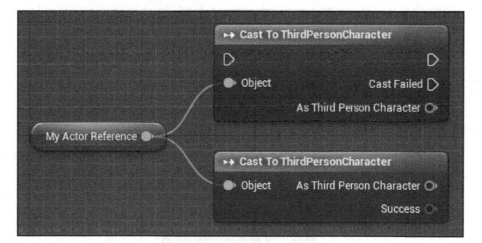

Casting object references

Type casting can be done in one of two ways. Dragging a connection off an object variable and typing `cast to` along with the desired class name will give you the most common casting node. You can see this in the Cast node in the top-right corner of this screenshot:

Very occasionally, you will need a pure cast (created by right-clicking the node on top and clicking **Convert to pure cast**), but be aware that the output may be null. It is safer to use the original version. Using the output execution pin on top guarantees that the reference is not null.

Class default variables

When working with subclasses, only the variables declared in that Blueprint will show up in the **Variables** section of the **My Blueprint** tab. For inherited non-private variables, you can press the **Class Defaults** button in the top toolbar to show them the **Details** tab on the right side. The variables declared in this Blueprint will also show up here, and all of them will be divided into sections based on the category we've set for them. A few sections worthy of examination include the following:

- **Default**: Any uncategorized variables will appear here, so this is the first place to look.
- **Rendering**: This controls the visibility of objects and to whom they are visible.
- **Replication**: This is discussed in greater detail in Chapter 7, *Multiplayer Games*. This section controls replication conditions for this actor.

Functions

Next, in the **My Blueprint** tab on the left-hand side, we will discuss functions (out of order I know, but important ones first).

To create a new function, hover over the plus sign next to functions in the **My Blueprint** tab. You will notice that two options appear: **Override** and **Function**. We will discuss Override in the next section with Events, so let's just click **Function** for now. A new tab will pop up with our new function's execution node:

The hollow white arrow here and on most other Blueprint nodes controls the flow of execution. Output arrows can only be connected to one place (if you need to do more than one thing, add a sequence node to specify the order), but input arrows can have more than one connection, as with the **GET** node here:

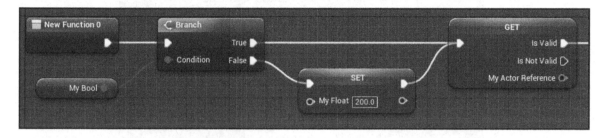

Note that not every output arrow needs to be connected to something. As soon as a function encounters the end of any set of instructions, it will return (unless you use output variables, as will be discussed shortly). For instance, in the preceding diagram, if **My Actor Reference** was null, the function's execution would stop there since nothing is connected to the **Is Not Valid** output.

One huge time saver when organizing your code is to double-click anywhere on a connection (this works for variable connections too) to create a reroute node.

In the following screenshot, I have used two reroute nodes beneath the Set node to avoid the false output passing through the Set node, which would make the function's flow harder to read:

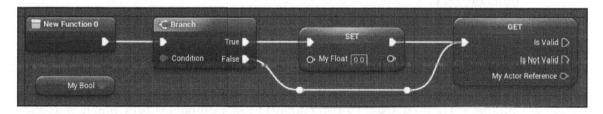

- When a function is selected in the **My Blueprints** tab on the left, the **Details** tab will appear on the right as it did with variables:

Most of these properties are simply for organizational purposes, but a few modify how the function works:

- **Description**: This will appear when you hover over the function name in the **My Blueprint** tab on the left-hand side.
- **Category**: As with Variables, this lets you organize functions into common themes in the **My Blueprints** tab.
- **Keywords**: In the same way that typing `if` in that pop-up window brings up the branch node, you can specify alternate keywords here to make searching for your function easier.
- **Compact Node Title**: Instead of having the full function name in the **Blueprint** window, you can specify an alternative name to be used for this function.
- **Access Specifier**: This stipulates whether this function is **Public**, **Protected**, or **Private**. Generally, it defaults to public.
- **Pure**: These types of functions have no execution pins and do not modify anything. These are useful when you just need a simple get-type function or one that performs a calculation without modifying any values itself. An example would be the first **Is Valid** node we looked at earlier when working with object reference variables.
- **Call In Editor**: This is useful for expanding the editor's capabilities, but this element won't be covered here.

Beneath these properties, we can add **Inputs** and **Outputs** variables:

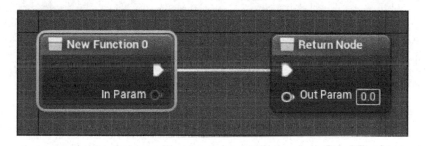

Pressing the plus sign next to **Inputs** or **Outputs** adds a new variable, while pressing **X** at the end of any variable removes it. You can use the arrow buttons to reorder variables, and, of course, specify its type using the drop-down list and icons next to them. These variables will appear on the input and output nodes in our function:

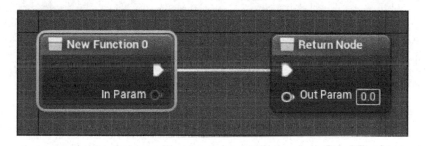

Note that while a function can only have one input node, you can duplicate the return node (by selecting it and pressing *Ctrl + W*, or by right-clicking anywhere and typing `return` into the **Search** box) as many times as you need.

Input variables have two additional properties that we can specify by pressing the arrow button to the left of the **Variable Name**:

- **Default Value**: When you add this function as a node elsewhere, this will appear as the default when nothing is plugged into the input for this variable.

- **Pass-By-Reference**: When this is checked, instead of passing in a value, this will pass in a reference to the variable itself. For example, say we had an RPG with stat numbers, such as strength and charisma, represented by floats. If we had an item that temporarily doubled a stat, we could have individual functions or an enum with a Select that specified which one we were working with, or we could simply use **Pass-By-Reference**. This will change the input node's variable to a diamond shape for easy identification. In this example, we would pass in any float variable and it would directly modify its value by doubling it:

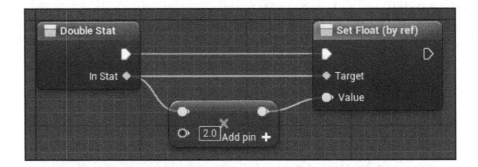

When using this function elsewhere, this input variable requires you to be connected, or you will receive a compiler error. Some default nodes use this functionality, such as the increment and decrement nodes for integers. Note the diamond-shaped input for the node in the following screenshot:

Local variables

While looking at a function in the main Blueprint window, an additional section appears on the **My Blueprints** tab on the left that stores the local variables for the current function. These can be added and altered in the same way as class-level variables, as well as having their default value set in the **Details** tab on the right-hand side.

Events

If we take a look at the **Event Graph** tab of the main Blueprint window (or double-click **Event Graph** in the **Graphs** section of the **My Blueprint** tab on the left-hand side), we'll see a bunch of code that looks like normal functions, but there is more than one function on this tab and they're red instead of purple. These are called *Events*:

These behave almost exactly like functions, but there are some key differences:

- Events can have latent actions, such as delay or download image, where the output pin is not immediately executed (similar to a yield in C#), whereas functions can not. These nodes will be indicated by a clock in the upper-right corner:

- Functions can use local variables; events cannot.
- Functions can have return value(s), events do not.
- Events can be replicated for multiplayer games, while functions cannot.
- You can also hook more than one event into the same block of code.

Events also have another extra bit of functionality. They can be used as delegates, which is where the red square in the upper-right corner comes in. Let's say that within a block of code, we wanted to set a timer and then do some other stuff. We could use the **Set Timer** node, and then drag a connection off the **Event** input and type `custom event` to create the delegate for that timer:

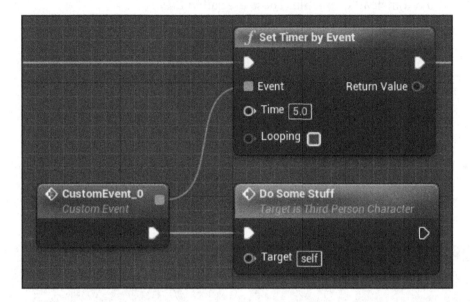

Once the timer is complete, our custom event will fire and execute the **Do Some Stuff** function that I have made up.

Overridable functions

To override a parent class function, hover over the plus sign next to **Functions** in the **My Blueprint** tab, and then press **Override**. Any non-private function or event in the parent blueprint can be overridden as displayed in the following screenshot:

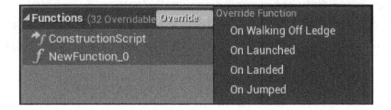

One quirk to this is that unless the overridden function has return values, it will appear as an event in the child blueprint, so you will lose the ability to use local variables unless you create a new function to pass everything from the overridden function to. Furthermore, although the overridden function now appears as an event, it will not have replication options.

If you need to call the parent function, just right-click on the node and select **Add call to parent function**, and then connect the event's output to the parent function call's input as follows:

Next, we will take a look at organizing a cluttered **Event** tab by using Graphs.

Graphs

Every Blueprint class will have an **Event Graph**, and when new Blueprints are created, they will have transparent nodes to give you a quick shortcut to three common events:

- **BeginPlay**: This is called after the object using this Blueprint has been initialized and play has begun for this object. Note that variables can still be null here, since players, HUDs, and other objects that are spawned at runtime may not have been spawned before this was called on others.
- **ActorBeginOverlap**: This is useful for detecting when a player has run into an item, for example.
- **Tick**: This is called every frame, and includes delta seconds so you can compensate for differences in frame rate.

The first three are optional and can be deleted if you don't need them.

In addition to the **Event Graph**, you can click on the plus sign next to Graphs on the left-hand side to create a new one. This is useful for organizing events such as Input (which we will discuss in a bit) into their own graph as these can quickly become cluttered.

One final aspect of the Blueprint window that we need to talk about is adding components to our Blueprint classes.

Components

Components are packages of code that provide common functionality in UE4, like lego blocks that we can use to build our Blueprints. Some of them provide physical parameters, such as skeletal meshes or particle effects, some provide physical elements, such as character or projectile movement, and some even provide simple things, such as an arrow to show which way the actor is facing in the editor or an icon we can use to differentiate between actors placed in the level while working in the editor.

We can see our Blueprints' component hierarchy in the **Components** tab in the top-left corner of our Blueprint window. We can also see how our Blueprint looks visually in the **Viewport** tab of the main Blueprint window (or by double-clicking any component to open the **Viewport** tab if it has been closed).

Now, let's take a look at our **ThirdPersonCharacter** components to get an idea of how they work:

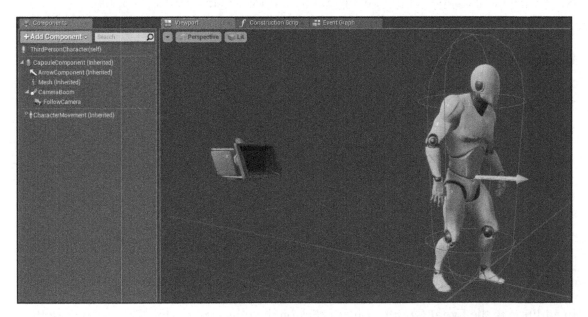

We can see that the root component of our character is a **CapsuleComponent**, which acts as the collision for our character. Attached to this root component are an **ArrowComponent**, to show us which direction the character is facing (useful when swapping out meshes to make sure they're still facing the correct direction), a **Mesh**, which, in this case, is a **SkeletalMeshComponent** that defines the actual physical body of the character that appears in game, and a **CameraBoom** (`SpringArmComponent`), which itself has a **FollowCamera** (`CameraComponent`) attached.

Beneath this, is our **CharacterMovement** component, which is a non-scene component and isn't part of the main hierarchy, but is still added to this Blueprint class.

One thing you may notice about components is that they themselves are variables and are inherited by child Blueprint classes. We can see this in most of the components here, and they have "(Inherited)" specified after their name in the hierarchy.

Like variables, components cannot be removed from child classes, so it is important to consider this when creating your class structure. They can, however, be hidden, both in game and in the editor if you need to.

Common components

Now, let's take a look at some of the more commonly used components in UE4 and what properties to look out for while using them (as always, these will show up in the **Details** panel on the right-hand side when a component is selected):

- **Static Mesh Component**: This is a normal mesh with no bones. It could be used for the visuals of a pickup, as a hat for our character, or for any number of things. When this isn't the root component, you can use the Transform properties to change the location, rotation, and scale of this component relative to the Blueprint itself. With a Static Mesh defined, you can also set custom materials in the section beneath it, which will override the default materials for that static mesh for this Blueprint. The **Collision** section defines how this component reacts to contact with other objects. The **Generate Overlap Events** checkbox provides us with special events for that component in the **Event Graph** tab, and the **Collision Presets** let us customize each individual collision reaction, depending on the type of object we've set it to. Further down, we have the **Lighting** section, which lets us specify which types of lighting affect this component and whether or not it casts a shadow. The next section, **Rendering**, controls whether this object is visible or not, or whether it is just *Hidden in Game* (this is what is toggled when using the **Set Actor Hidden In Game** node shown earlier in this chapter). There are also two important ones hidden in the advanced properties by pressing the down arrow in the **Rendering** section: **Owner No See** and **Only Owner See**, which come into play when working on multiplayer games.

- **Skeletal Mesh Component**: This is a mesh with bones that can be animated. A lot of the properties of this type of component are the same as a static mesh component, but there is one additional section to talk about. In the **Animation** section, we can specify a single asset (for example, a simple animated piece of machinery) or a more complicated animation blueprint that responds to changing variables. Animation blueprints will be discussed in more detail in Chapter 5, *Animation Blueprints*.

- **Box, Capsule, and Sphere Collision**: This is a simplified collision used as an optimization. Instead of having per-poly collision for an object simply moving around, we can use a simplified collision. Note that this doesn't necessarily replace what most people call hitboxes. Collisions calculated during weapon firing can ignore this simplified collision if desired.

- **Particle System and Audio Components**: While not strictly necessary to be able to play sounds and spawn particle effects, if those are part of what this Blueprint *is*, as opposed to something it sometimes *does*, you can use these components as a more permanent place for them.

- **Movement Components**: Four simple types of movement components are provided here. **Floating Pawn** is appropriate for flying vehicle type physics, while **Interp To**, **Projectile**, and **Rotating** are more appropriate for objects instead of characters. You may notice that **Character Movement Component** is not selectable in this list. That type of component is native to, and inherited by, character subclasses only. The other types of movement components have their own sections for speed, friction, and so on, that define its properties.

- **Text Render**: This allows you to render text as part of an object in game. Font, color, outline, and other properties can be adjusted, and the text can be changed at runtime.

- **Widget**: This allows you to add a UI component to this Blueprint, like an interactable keypad on a door. Creating UIs will be discussed in Chapter 4, *Creating HUDs and Menus Using UMG*, but advanced topics, such as an interactable door, are not part of that. However, there are a lot of tutorials available for advanced topics such as this.

Components may need to be attached as child components to others in order to get the desired functionality. In our `ThirdPersonCharacter` blueprint, this can be seen with the `CameraBoom` and `FollowCamera` components. For example, if we had a static mesh component we wanted to use as a hat, we would drag it onto the Mesh component to set it as a child of that. When this is done, we can use the Parent Socket property under the **Sockets** section to specify where it should be attached (in this case, clicking the magnifying glass icon and selecting 'head' would suffice).

Once the component is properly attached, we can use the location, rotation, and scale properties in the **Transform** section to move it to where we would like it to be.

Component events

Each component type has its own set of events that can be called for that component. For example, if we select the Mesh component and go back into the Event Graph of the main Blueprint window, we can right-click and see a special section at the top with events specific to that component:

These overlap events can be used, for example, to pick up an item on the ground when you walk into it, but it would be better to do this in the pickup class itself, which we will do in a bit.

Now that we've covered variables, events, functions, graphs, and components, now is a good time to put all of this to use in some practical examples.

Time for action

Our awesome game has been sitting there not getting awesome, so let's start expanding it with some Blueprints of our own.

The first thing we will do is add a sprint button for our character. This will cover a lot of the things we've discussed in this chapter, as well as the previous one:

1. Go back to the main editor window.
2. Go to **Edit** | **Project Settings**, and scroll down to the **Engine** section.
3. Click on the **Input** subsection.
4. Press the plus sign next to **Action Mappings** and name the new one Sprint.

5. Assign it a key of **Left Shift**:

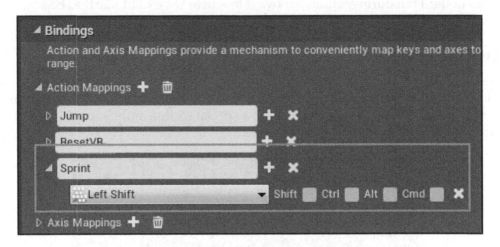

6. Close the **Project Settings** page and go back to out `ThirdPersonCharacter`'s main blueprint window and the **Event Graph** tab.

7. Right-click and type `Sprint`. Our custom input event will show up as an option:

8. Now, go to the **Components** tab on the left and drag the **Character Movement** component out into the main window to create a reference to it.

9. Once that's done, drag a connection off its output, type `walk speed`, and then select **Set Max Walk Speed**.

Be careful not to accidentally select **SET Max Walk Speed**, an easy mistake to make that still trips me up every once in a while

10. Select that new node and press *Ctrl + W* to duplicate it, or repeat the process of dragging a connection off the **Character Movement** variable to make a new one.

11. Once both are created, connect one of them to the **Pressed** output of our sprint event, and the other one to the **Released** output.

If we select our **Character Movement** component on the left side and take a look at its properties on the right, in the **Character Movement**: Walking section, we can see that our default **Max Walk Speed** is 600. With this in mind, let's set the **Pressed** output's **Max Walk Speed** to 2000, and the **Released** output's back down to 600. We should have a Blueprint script that looks something like this:

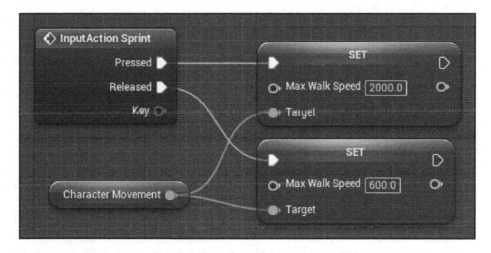

Now, we can compile the Blueprint by pressing the **Compile** button in the top toolbar, which should have an orange question mark by now. If you've been experimenting with any functions or variables that are causing a compiler error at this point, double-clicking on the errors in the **Compiler Results** tab at the bottom will take you to them. But for now, I'd just delete them.

Once the code compiles and the button shows a green check mark, press the **Play** button, either here or back in the main editor window (make sure the down arrow next to it has **New Editor Window** selected), and we can see by holding the left shift key, that our sprint code works! Awesome.

Creating a Blueprint from scratch

Now, let's give our character something to do. We're going to create a pickup that changes the character's material to the pickup's material:

1. In the main editor window's **Content Browser** at the bottom, go into the ThirdPersonBP\Blueprints folder where our ThirdPersonCharacter is.

2. Right-click and select Blueprint class, and then select **Actor** as our parent class to finish creating the new Blueprint asset. For proper object-oriented programming techniques, let's name it BasePickup so that we can easily add other pickup types later.

3. With that created, double-click the Blueprint to open it up. We'll notice that our **Components** tab is empty, except for the DefaultSceneRoot, which, as a base scene component, has very few properties and is invisible in game. Our Blueprint is a blank slate.

4. To change that, press **Add Component** in the top left and select **Sphere**, which is a programmer-art shortcut to adding a static mesh component with a default sphere mesh already assigned.

5. For the material, go back into the **Content Browser** of the main editor window and enter the StarterContent\Materials folder (if you didn't add the starter content, refer to Chapter 1, *Introduction to Unreal Engine 4*, for adding it to an existing project). Select the M_Ground_Moss material, and, back in our BasePickup Blueprint window, make sure the **Sphere** component is still selected and press the left arrow in the **Materials** section to assign it. (If you have enough window space, you can also drag the material directly from the **Content Browser** into this property.)

6. By default, this sphere will block our player from walking through it, so, with the **Sphere** component selected, let's go over to the Details tab on the right-hand side and, in the **Collision** section, change the collision presets to OverlapAllDynamic. This will allow the player to walk through it, and provide access to the event we need in order to detect that. With all that done, we should have a Blueprint that looks something like this:

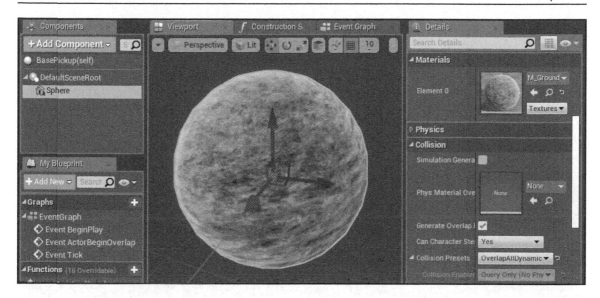

Now, we'll take a second here to compile and then save our Blueprint. Save on a frequent basis:

7. In the **Event Graph** tab, we can delete the three default events as we will not be using them (you can drag a box to select all of them at once). Instead, with the **Sphere** component selected, right-click anywhere in this graph and click **Add Event For Sphere** | **Collision** | **Add On Component Begin Overlap**.

8. This event has quite a few variables, but the only one we're concerned with for now is **Other Actor**. We want to make sure that only the player can pick this up, so let's drag a connection off here and cast it to `ThirdPersonCharacter`. You'll notice that, when we do this, it will automatically connect the execution output to this new node, which is handy.

9. Now, we'll create a base function to handle being picked up. Over in the **My Blueprint** tab on the left, add a new function and call it `HandlePickedUp`. We'll give it one input variable, a `ThirdPersonCharacter` variable named `PickedUpBy`. We won't do anything else with this function in the base class, so we're done with this function for now:

At this point, we need to compile our Blueprint; otherwise, the input variable may be incorrectly named `New Param` when we try to call this function and we will get an error:

10. Back in the main **Event Graph**, we can now call this function after our cast. Drag the execution pin off and start typing `HandlePickedUp` until our custom function shows up, and add it. Also, connect the variable output from the cast to it. Our **Event Graph** should now look like this:

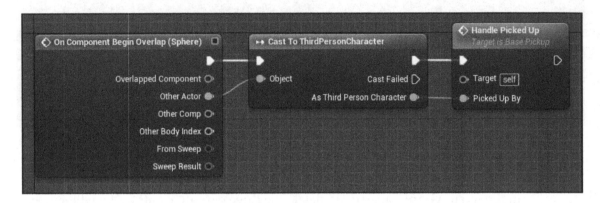

With that done, compile and save this Blueprint and we're done with this class. Let's now close out this Blueprint's window.

One small material change

Unfortunately, for all of this to work, we will have to dive a tiny bit into some art assets. By default, the materials included with the starter content will only work on static mesh components, so, for us to be able to apply them to our character, we will need to take a quick second to check a few boxes.

In the **Content Browser**, navigate back to the `StarterContent\Materials` folder. Double-click on the `M_Ground_Moss` asset to open it up, and, in the **Details** tab in the bottom-left corner, scroll down to the **Usage** section and check the **Used With Skeletal Mesh** box:

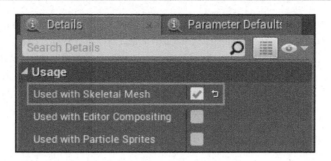

Once that's done, click the **Save** button at the top of this window, and, once it's done saving, close the window.

We'll want a few materials to switch between, so, in the same folder of the **Content Browser**, repeat the process of checking the skeletal mesh box and saving with M_Metal_Gold and M_Wood_Oak materials.

That should be sufficient for our purposes, so we're done with the art assets. Now, let's create a child of our BasePickup class with some actual functionality.

Creating a child Blueprint

Back in the **Content Browser**, right-click on our BasePickup class and select **Create Child Blueprint Class**. Let's name this one Pickup_MaterialSwitcher, and open it up.

We can see that our components have been inherited along with their properties. Now, all we need to do is override the HandlePickedUp function. In the **My Blueprint** tab on the left-hand side, hover over the plus sign next to **Functions** and look in the **Override** list for **Handle Picked Up**. Remember that because our function has no return value, this overridden function will appear as an event in our **Event Graph** tab.

The functionality for this one will be simple. Drag a connection off the **Picked Up By** variable input and type mesh to find the **Get Mesh** option. This will create the mesh variable. Drag a connection off that and type set material to create a Set Material node, and connect the execution pin from our Handle Picked Up event to it.

Only two more nodes are required. First, grab the **Sphere** component from our **Components** tab and drag it into the graph, and then drag the output and type `get material` to create a Get Material node. Connect its return value output to the material input of our Set Material node and we're done. You'll notice that both the set and Get Material nodes have an element index input as well, but, since we'll only be changing the first material anyway, we can ignore those and leave them at their default of `0`.

Our **Event Graph** should look like this:

We're finished with our Blueprint classes, so we can compile and close this Blueprint's window. Now for the fun part!

Back in the main editor window, move the camera to get a good view of the `ThirdPersonExampleMap`'s floor. Now, let's drag our `Pickup_MaterialSwitcher` Blueprint into the level and place three of them in different locations.

With them placed, we'll want to change two of them to use different materials to our default moss. Select one of them, and, in the **Details** tab on the right, select the **Sphere** component. (It may be hard to see and you may need to expand the components section. It is right beneath the **Add Component** button.) In the **Content Browser**, head over to `StarterContent\Materials` and drag the `M_Metal_Gold` material into the **Element 0** slot for our component. This will turn that instance of the Blueprint gold. Do the same with the third instance and the `M_Wood_Oak` material.

Now, our level should look something like this:

Once our Blueprints have been placed, we're ready to play the level. Run into the spheres and our character's material should change to match each one:

Awesome!

Giving our game a goal

Now our character has something to do, but let's expand this a bit further and hook in the GameMode class to give our game an end condition. We'll make the pickups disappear when you run into them, and have the game exit a few seconds after you pick up the last one.

1. First up, have GameMode track the pickups. In the **Content Browser**, in the ThirdPersonBP\Blueprints folder, double-click ThirdPersonGameMode to open it up.
2. You'll immediately notice that this class looks a lot different than the other Blueprint classes we've used. When a Blueprint class contains no code, the editor will show the class in this compacted view with just the **Class Defaults** showing for the variables. Since we want to add some code, click the **Open Full Blueprint Editor** link in this window to get back to a normal view.
3. To keep track of our pickups, let's add a new variable, an int called **RemainingPickups**.
4. Now, we need to get a count of how many of our pickups are in the level. In the **Event Graph**, right-click and type begin play to get the **BeginPlay** event. This will run as soon as the level starts up.
5. Drag a connection off and type All Actors to get a Get All Actors of Class node. In this node's actor class dropdown, type in basepickup to select our BasePickup class (not just our material switcher subclass).
6. The output of this node will be an array containing all of the found actors of that class. If we wanted to do something specific to each of them, we could drag the output variable off and make a ForEach node, but here we only need to get the array length, so drag a connection off the array variable output and type length to get the Array Length node.
7. By way of a final step, drag a connection off that int and type in RemainingPickups to set it to the array length.

   Our class should now look like this:

8. Now, we need to keep track of when one is picked up. Instead of using a function, for now, let's just use an event for this. Right-click beneath the BeginPlay code somewhere and type in custom event to create a Custom Event node. Name it PickupCollected.

9. Drag our RemainingPickups int into the **Event Graph**, and then drag a connection off it and type decrement to subtract one from our int every time this event fires.

10. Out of the Decrement node, drag a connection off and type less to get a Less Than or Equal node (the or equal part is important here), and leave the other pin at its default of 0.

11. Drag a connection off the output Boolean and type if to get the Branch node, and then connect the execution input to our PickupCollected event.

Let's pause here to make sure our code looks like this so far:

12. Once the number of pickups drops to **0**, let's exit the game. To do this, drag a connection off the **True** output of the branch and type set timer to create a **Set Timer by Event** node.

13. Drag a connection off the event input of the timer node and type custom to create a custom event, and name it GameFinished. Set the time on the timer node to 3 seconds.

14. Finally, drag a connection off our GameFinished event and type in console to create a console command node. This node lets us input commands and should be familiar to anyone who has used the tilde key (~) to input cheats or other commands into different games.

15. For the command, set it to quit (without the quote marks).

Our code should now look like this:

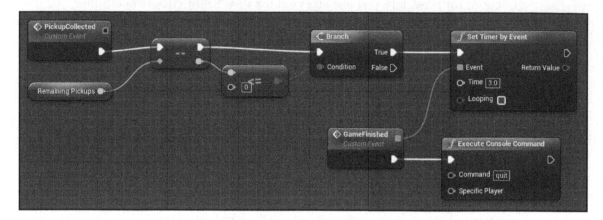

We're done with the GameMode class, so we can close this window and reopen our BasePickup class. We'll be working in our HandlePickedUp function here, so double-click on that in the left-hand side to open up that tab in the main window:

1. First, we need a reference to the GameMode, so right-click anywhere in here and type game mode to find the **Get Game Mode node**. We'll need to cast that to our game mode, so drag a connection and type cast to cast it to ThirdPersonGameMode. Connect the execution pins of our two nodes.

2. Now, drag a connection off the **As Third Person Game Mode** output and type pickup to get our custom PickupCollected event call. Finally, drag a connection off the output execution pin and type destroy to get the **Destroy Actor** node, so this pickup will disappear when we collect it.

Our code should now look like this:

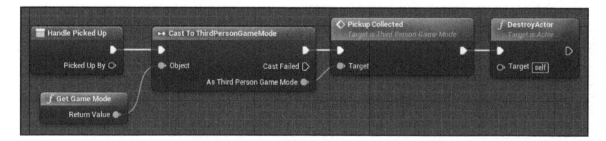

We're done in the base class, so we can close this.

There is now only one event left to create before we can test this out:

1. Open up our `Pickup_MaterialSwitcher` class and take a look at the **Event Graph**. Since we're overriding the `HandlePickedUp` function, we'll need to add a call to the parent function for that code to work, so right-click on the `HandlePickedUp` event and click **Add Call to Parent Function**.

2. Move this to the end of the code (we need our code to execute before the parent function destroys the actor) and connect it.

3. Don't forget to also connect the **Picked Up By** input variable all the way to the end. We can double-click on the line to create reroute nodes to make the code cleaner.

Now we're done, and our material switcher code should look like this:

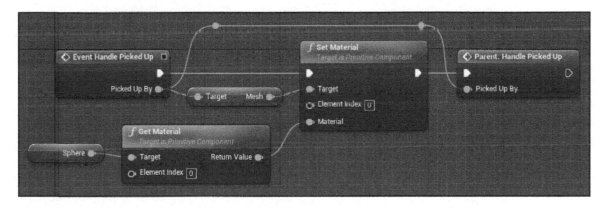

Compile and close this Blueprint, and then hit the **Play** button to test all of this out. Run around collecting the pickups, which should still switch your character's material before they disappear. Once all three have been collected, the window should automatically close after three seconds.

Summary

We've covered a lot in this chapter, and I hope I've cleared up any confusion you've had over the way Blueprints are used. As you can see, they are an incredibly powerful tool, and by browsing the nodes in the right-click menu, you can see that practically everything you want to do can be done in Blueprints as an alternative to traditional code.

You can quite easily create entire games using nothing but Blueprint code. In the next chapter, however, we will discuss adding C++ code to a Blueprint project for those rare instances when Blueprint alone is not enough.

3
Adding C++ to a Blueprint Project

Sometimes, try as you might, adding C++ to your Blueprint project will be unavoidable. Maybe you have a complex function that needs to run every frame and it's impacting your game's performance. Maybe you've encountered a rare case where some of the engine's functionality isn't exposed to Blueprint, such as creating a key bind menu. Or perhaps you're working on a non-game project that needs to hook into some exterior systems.

Or maybe you just prefer to work in C++. Even in this case, there may still be times when you need to interact with the Blueprint system, so knowing how these systems interact will help with your game's development.

Back in Chapter 1, *Introduction to Unreal Engine 4*, we talked about the ability to add C++ to an existing Blueprint project and vice versa. In this chapter, we will go over that, as well as discuss how to expose your custom C++ functionality to Blueprints if you need that ability.

The following topics will be covered in this chapter:

- Creating and using C++ Classes in UE4
- Using C++ variables and functions in Blueprint
- Creating custom Blueprint events in C++

Technical requirements

To get up and running with C++, we'll need to install Visual Studio. As of the time of writing, we will need the 2017 version. If your project uses an Unreal Engine version other than the 4.21 version we're using, you can check which Visual Studio you need in Epic's documentation here: https://docs.unrealengine.com/en-us/Programming/Development/VisualStudioSetup.

Always check Epic's UE4 version release notes for changes in the Visual Studio version, especially if you want or need to update your project's engine version to take advantage of new features.

You can download and install a free version of Visual Studio from Microsoft's website (https://visualstudio.microsoft.com/).

If you already have another version of Visual Studio installed, your code may open in the wrong version, or you may have updated and wish to change the version. If this is the case, you can change it by going into the editor and then going to **Edit** | **Editor Preferences** and looking in the **Source Code Editor** section:

Once you have Visual Studio installed, reopen the **AwesomeGame** project in the editor and prepare for some programming.

Creating C++ classes in UE4

To create our first C++ class, right-click in the asset panel of the **Content Browser** (or click **Add New** at the top left of it) and click **New C++ Class...**:

Unlike the usual UE4 assets, our C++ code will reside in a folder outside **Content**, so it won't matter which asset folder you're currently in when you add a **New C++ Class**.

Now, we need to decide what to extend from. Most of the time, we'll be working with `Actor` classes (including **Pawn**, **PlayerController**, and **GameMode**), and the most commonly extended classes will appear in the list that pops up:

While scrolling down the list, you will find that there are also other useful classes to extend from, including the **heads-up display (HUD)** and slate widgets (both discussed in `Chapter 4, Creating HUDs and Menus Using UMG`) and Blueprint function libraries.

If we need to extend from a class that isn't in this common list, we can click on the **Show All Classes** button to get the full list of classes in a hierarchy view. This list is pretty extensive, and it can be difficult to locate the class you want to extend, so there is a **Search** bar at the top:

For our custom class, we'll just be extending from **Actor**, so make sure the **Show All Classes** box is unchecked and select **Actor**, which should be the fourth one down:

Click **Next**, and the **Name Your New Actor** dialogue will come up. Here, we can set the name of our new class as well as the location:

There are also options for changing the module for the code if we're creating more than one. Most projects won't, and we only have one at the moment anyway, so we can ignore this.

The other option lets us make this class **Public** or **Private**. By default, it will be **Public**, so we don't need to do anything here either.

We will also keep the `MyActor` name for our class.

Press the **Create Class** button at the bottom and give the editor a minute or two to add the necessary files to our project and then compile the code. Once this is done, the editor will launch Visual Studio and we can get our first look at C++ in Unreal Engine 4.

First, we will look at the `.cpp` class:

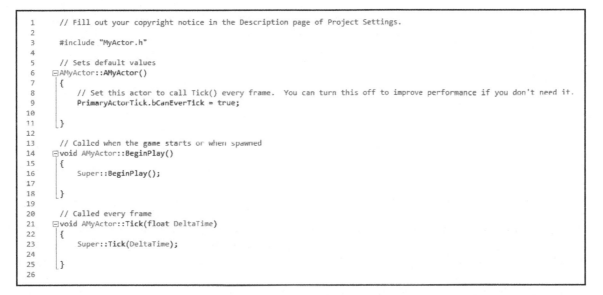

By default, three common functions are included with newly created C++ classes in UE4:

1. The first is the constructor, where we can set any default variables we need as well as set up components this class will use.
2. The next is `BeginPlay`, which is called when the game has started and play begins. This is useful for actions that need to be taken when all objects in the level have been loaded and initialized, or for initializing newly spawned actors during play. For example, if we needed to store this actor's initial location or grab references to other actors or objects, we would do it here.
3. The last of the three is `Tick`, which is called every frame. This varies with `framerate`, so `DeltaTime` is included so that you can compensate for this where needed.

Next, we'll take a look at the `.h` file:

```
1      // Fill out your copyright notice in the Description page of Project Settings.
2
3      #pragma once
4
5    #include "CoreMinimal.h"
6      #include "GameFramework/Actor.h"
7      #include "MyActor.generated.h"
8
9      UCLASS()
10   class AWESOMEGAME_API AMyActor : public AActor
11   {
12       GENERATED_BODY()
13
14   public:
15       // Sets default values for this actor's properties
16       AMyActor();
17
18   protected:
19       // Called when the game starts or when spawned
20       virtual void BeginPlay() override;
21
22   public:
23       // Called every frame
24       virtual void Tick(float DeltaTime) override;
25
26   };
```

Here, we can see two macros: UCLASS() and GENERATED_BODY(), which are used by the engine to set up our class to work with UE4. After this, we have the headers for the three functions we saw in the `.cpp` file.

Next, let's take a look at how to use this class in the editor.

Using C++ classes in UE4

Now that we have our C++ class set up, the remainder of this chapter will focus on interaction between C++ and Blueprint classes and how to expose different functionality to Blueprints from our C++ classes.

To start, let's learn how to extend from our C++ classes with Blueprints. To do this, we'll simply set up a print statement in C++ that we'll be able to see in a placed Blueprint class.

First, we need to set up our C++ code. We won't need the Tick function, so we can delete that from both the `.cpp` and `.h` files, and delete the PrimaryActorTick line from the constructor in the `.cpp` file.

For the print statement, we will use UE4's version, which is UE_LOG(). There are a few parameters dealing with the type of log that it is, so we'll set it as a warning so it will stand out in the log window:

```
UE_LOG(LogTemp, Warning, TEXT("OUR C++ CLASS IS WORKING!"));
```

The BeginPlay function in our .cpp file should now look like this:

```
// Called when the game starts or when spawned
void AMyActor::BeginPlay()
{
    Super::BeginPlay();

    UE_LOG(LogTemp, Warning, TEXT("OUR C++ CLASS IS WORKING!"));
}
```

Save both files, and now we have two options to compile our code. We can do it directly in Visual Studio with the **Build** button, or we can use the **Compile** button in the top toolbar in the Unreal Editor. Either way we handle it, the resulting compiled code will be hot reloaded by the editor, so we won't have to restart it every time we compile our code.

Compile the code and head into the editor. Our C++ classes will appear in the **Content Browser**, but not in the Content folder. It will be in the C++ Classes folder:

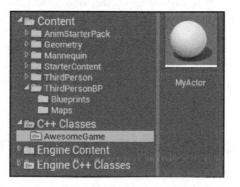

If you don't see the C++ Classes folder, click on the **View Options** button in the bottom right of the **Content Browser** (it has an eyeball symbol next to it) and make sure that **C++ Classes** is checked.

Now, let's run a quick test of our log output. If we drag the MyActor class into the level viewport, we can place an instance of it. It will not be visible or have the transform widget because it does not have any components. We will be able to see it in the **World Outliner** tab on the right-hand side of the editor, though.

With that in place, go to **Window** | **Developer Tool**s | **Output Log** to bring up the log window. Right-click and hit **Clear Log** to make it easier for our new code to see, and then hit the **Play** button in the top toolbar of the main editor window to run the game. We can hit *Esc* to close it out as soon as it starts running since our `BeginPlay` code will show up immediately:

```
LogWorld: Bringing up level for play took: 0.00257
LogContentBrowser: Native class hierarchy updated
LogTemp: Warning: OUR C++ CLASS IS WORKING!
PIE: Play in editor start time for /Game/ThirdPers
LogBlueprintUserMessages: Late PlayInEditor Detect
```

Now that our code is working, let's make a Blueprint class that extends from our C++ class. We'll use this class to demonstrate the interaction between C++ and Blueprints.

First, delete the `MyActor` instance from the level. Select it in the **World Outliner** tab on the right of the editor window and press **Delete** to get rid of it. We'll be using a Blueprint subclass of `MyActor`, which we'll create now.

In the **Content Browser**, go to the `ThirdPersonBP\Blueprints` folder where we've placed all of our Blueprint code so far. Click the **Add New** button and select **Blueprint Class**. In the **Pick Parent Class** window that comes up, type `MyActor` in the **Search** bar and select it. Press the **Select** button to create the Blueprint, and name it `MyActor_Blueprint` (the name doesn't matter; this is just so we can easily keep track of it).

Now, if we drag the `MyActor_Blueprint` into the level, we can see the default `SceneComponent` sphere-shaped sprite as well as the transform gizmo. If we repeat the test of pressing **Play** in the top toolbar, we'll see the same log output as before. Perfect!

Using C++ variables in Blueprint

Now that both our C++ class and Blueprint subclass are set up, we can take a look at how they can interact. First up, let's add a variable in C++ that we can use in Blueprint.

In our `MyActor.h` file in Visual Studio, we can add variables as we normally would. Unreal has a few custom variable types, such as using an `FString` instead of a standard string, but for now we'll just use a float.

If we simply declared a float in our header file, it would not be accessible in Blueprints. For that, we need to use a special UE4 macro, UPROPERTY. Using this, we can specify where and how our variable can be used. Most commonly, variables exposed to Blueprint need to be accessible anywhere (class defaults, in the Blueprint code itself, and in the level instance properties), as well as be readable and writable.

Let's add a float called TestFloat to our header file and add these properties to it using EditAnywhere and BlueprintReadWrite in the UPROPERTY:

```
UCLASS()
class AWESOMEGAME_API AMyActor : public AActor
{
    GENERATED_BODY()

public:
    UPROPERTY(EditAnywhere, BlueprintReadWrite)
        float TestFloat;

public:
    // Sets default values for this actor's properties
    AMyActor();

protected:
    // Called when the game starts or when spawned
    virtual void BeginPlay() override;

};
```

Compile our code and head back into the editor. If we open up our MyActor_Blueprint, it should be in data-only mode with the class default variables showing. We can see the TestFloat variable there under the MyActor section.

Click on **Open Full Blueprint Editor**. In this window, we can see that TestFloat doesn't show up under the Variables section on the left. This makes sense since parent variables only show up in the class defaults.

If we right-click in the Blueprint window and start typing 'Test Float', we can add both the **Get** and **Set** nodes for it:

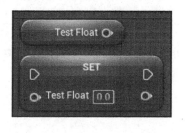

Now, we can use that variable as we would any other Blueprint variable, as well as use it in C++. Next, let's create a few different C++ functions that we can access in different ways through Blueprint.

Using C++ functions in Blueprint

There are several ways that we can expose C++ functions to Blueprint, depending on what we need them to do. For our first example, we're going to make a simple function that we pass our float variable to and get an output from. Let's open up our C++ files and get started.

BlueprintCallable functions

For this first test, we're going to make a `BlueprintCallable` function. These work like the function calls we made back in `Chapter 2`, *Programming Using Blueprints*, with `HandlePickedUp`, except the actual code is in C++.

Our function will simply take a float and double it and then return that value. In the `.cpp` file, this is what the C++ code will look like for that:

```
float AMyActor::DoubleValue(float InValue)
{
    return InValue * 2.f;
}
```

In the `.h` file, we will add the function as normal, but in order to use this function in Blueprint, we will need to use a macro similar to what we did with the variable. In this case, instead of a `UPROPERTY` we will use a `UFUNCTION` with a `BlueprintCallable` specifier:

```
public:
    UFUNCTION(BlueprintCallable)
    float DoubleValue(float InValue);
```

We're done in the C++ files for now, so let's save them and recompile the code.

Back in the editor, we can now use our `DoubleValue` function in Blueprint. Open our `MyActor_Blueprint` class again, right-click in the Blueprint window, and type `DoubleValue` in the search bar. Our function will appear and we can add it.

To test our function, let's hook it up to the `BeginPlay` event and connect its output to a `Print` function. Now, put a value for **In Value**, as I've done here with `256.0`:

Compile the Blueprint and open the log output window again (**Window** | **Developer Tools** | **Output Log**). Run the game and we'll see the result of our C++ code running through a Blueprint function call:

```
LogBlueprintUserMessages: [MyActor_Blueprint_5] 512.0
LogTemp: Warning: OUR C++ CLASS IS WORKING!
```

Next, we'll take a look at `BlueprintPure` functions.

BlueprintPure functions

Back in `Chapter 2`, *Programming Using Blueprints*, we discussed `Pure` functions. These are functions that have no execution pins and do not modify any values themselves. They are useful for `get` type functions, such as the `Get Material` we used for our pickup spheres.

For our pure function, we're going to do another simple calculation, but we'll use one of UE4's variable types in addition to a float. We'll take in an `FVector` and add a float to the height (`Z` variable).

In our `.cpp` file, the function should look like this:

```
FVector AMyActor::AddToHeight(FVector InLocation, float InAddHeight)
{
    FVector added = InLocation;
    added.Z += InAddHeight;
    return added;
}
```

Note that local variables are OK to use in pure functions; we just won't be doing anything to class variables such as `TestFloat`.

For the `.h` file, in addition to making the `BlueprintPure` function, we're also going to add a category specifier. This helps us to organize our C++ functions when accessible in Blueprint. Using the | key (hold shift and press the backslash key), we can add subcategories for our function.

Here is what the addition to our header file should look like:

```
public:
    UFUNCTION(BlueprintPure, Category = "Math|AwesomeGame")
    FVector AddToHeight(FVector InLocation, float InAddHeight);
```

This will make our function show up under the `Math|AwesomeGame` category.

Now, we can compile our code and head back into the editor. Open up our `MyActor_Blueprint` class again and let's delete everything connected to the **BeginPlay** Event.

Now, let's add our new pure function. Right-click and find it under **Math | Awesome Game**:

We can see that our two input variables show up on the left side, and the output on the right. Note that since this is a pure function, unlike our `DoubleValue` one, this one does not have execution pins:

Now, we need to test it out. We could just plug in some values for the input, but let's go a few steps further:

1. Hook up a GetActorLocation function to the InLocation input, and TestFloat to the InAddHeight input.
2. Make a new Print function and hook it into the BeginPlay function.
3. Drag a connection from the InString input of the Print function and add an **Append** node.
4. Press the **Add Pin** button on the **Append** node twice to add two new inputs for it.
5. In the first input, type BEFORE: and be sure to include a space after it to separate it from the next input.
6. For the next input, drag a connection from the GetActorLocation's output and connect it to append's second input. This will automatically create a vector-to-string converter in-between them.
7. For the third input, type AFTER: and be sure to include spaces both before and after this to separate it from the other inputs.
8. For the last input, drag a connection from the Return Value of our AddToHeight node. This will also automatically add the vector-to-string converter.
9. There is now one last step. Since our test float's default value is zero, we need to press the **Class Defaults** button at the top of the Blueprint window (or select the TestFloat node) and change the value in the panel on the right side of the **Blueprint** window. To make it simple, I've set it to 100.

This is what our Blueprint code should look like now:

Compile our Blueprint, and then open up the output log window. Now, when we run our game, the result of our `AddToHeight` code will show up with the values both before and after the calculation so that we can compare them to make sure it is working properly:

```
BEFORE: X=-570.000 Y=150.000 Z=190.000  AFTER: X=-570.000 Y=150.000 Z=290.000
```

We can see that the `Z` value increased by 100, so our code is working!

Now, what if we need more than one variable output? We can easily do this with `out` variables, and this will work for both normal and pure function calls.

Using out variables in C++

We're going to be making two new functions for this. Both will have the same code to keep it simple, but one will be a normal function and the other will be a pure version. Let's make it both add to, and subtract from, the height and output both.

Let's start with the `.cpp` file. The code here is fairly simple:

```cpp
void AMyActor::AddAndSubtractHeight(FVector InLocation, float InHeight, FVector& OutAdded, FVector& OutSubtracted)
{
    OutAdded = InLocation;
    OutAdded.Z += InHeight;
    OutSubtracted = InLocation;
    OutSubtracted.Z -= InHeight;
}

void AMyActor::AddAndSubtractHeight_Pure(FVector InLocation, float InHeight, FVector& OutAdded, FVector& OutSubtracted)
{
    OutAdded = InLocation;
    OutAdded.Z += InHeight;
    OutSubtracted = InLocation;
    OutSubtracted.Z -= InHeight;
}
```

Note that the `out` variables are references (ampersand (`&`) symbol after the type).

Now, let's add the functions to our header file:

```cpp
public:
    UFUNCTION(BlueprintCallable, Category = "Math|AwesomeGame")
    void AddAndSubtractHeight(FVector InLocation, float InHeight, FVector& OutAdded, FVector& OutSubtracted);

    UFUNCTION(BlueprintPure, Category = "Math|AwesomeGame")
    void AddAndSubtractHeight_Pure(FVector InLocation, float InHeight, FVector& OutAdded, FVector& OutSubtracted);
```

This is pretty simple. The actual function declarations are the same except the name, and except the UFUNCTION lines that have a different Blueprint specifier.

Compile our C++ code and head back into the editor. Since we've added both of our new functions to the same **Math | Awesome Game** category as our previous one, they'll be easy to find:

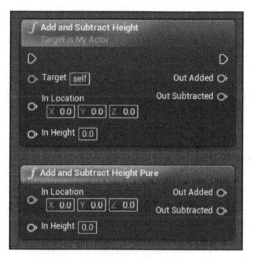

Next, let's take a look at how to add our own Event call.

Using events in C++

Most of the events we've been using, such as BeginPlay and Tick, are called from C++. We've taken a look at how to create our own in Blueprints, and now we'll see how to create them in C++ for use in our own Blueprints.

For this, we will start in the header file. Events are created much the same way our normal and pure functions were, but we use the BlueprintImplementableEvent specifier. We'll also add an output float that we can log:

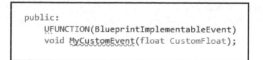

```cpp
public:
    UFUNCTION(BlueprintImplementableEvent)
    void MyCustomEvent(float CustomFloat);
```

For this one, we won't implement the function in the `.cpp` file, so ignore the green line under the function name.

In the `.cpp` file, we'll add a call to our custom Event in the `BeginPlay` function to keep it simple. We just need to add one line at the end, and we'll hardcode a value of `256` for the output:

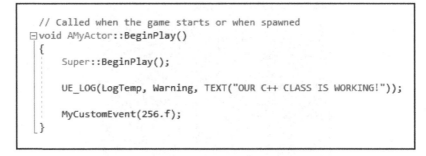

```cpp
// Called when the game starts or when spawned
void AMyActor::BeginPlay()
{
    Super::BeginPlay();

    UE_LOG(LogTemp, Warning, TEXT("OUR C++ CLASS IS WORKING!"));

    MyCustomEvent(256.f);
}
```

That's all we need for the C++ side of things, so compile the code and head back into the editor.

Delete all of our existing Blueprint code from `MyActor_Blueprint`, and add our custom `MyCustomEvent` Event. From the output, create a `Print` function call and hook our `CustomFloat` output to its `InString` input. Our Blueprint code should look like this:

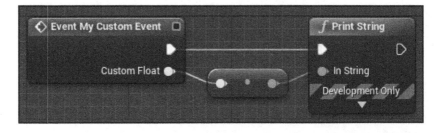

Compile our Blueprint, and then run the game. We'll see our hardcoded value outputted in the log:

```
LogTemp: Warning: OUR C++ CLASS IS WORKING!
LogBlueprintUserMessages: [MyActor_Blueprint_5] 256.0
```

Summary

The decision to use C++ or Blueprints in your project is down to personal preference in most cases. Sometimes, you will need the speed advantages that C++ provides. Sometimes, you will need some functionality that Blueprints don't provide by default.

Most complex projects will most likely end up with both C++ and Blueprint code. For this reason, it's important to know how they interact, and how to get access to the C++ side of things from Blueprints. I hope this chapter has helped with that.

Next up, we will take a look at UE4's **UMG** system to create menus and an HUD for our `AwesomeGame` project.

4
Creating HUDs and Menus Using UMG

Now that we have some semblance of a newly built game, we need to take the next step and start adding a UI to *Awesome Game*. Unreal Engine has a system called **Unreal motion graphics (UMG)**, which it uses to make interfaces. This is accomplished through the use of widgets, which are premade UI elements, such as buttons, images, and sliders. We can use these elements to build our **heads-up displays (HUDs)** and menus.

Using UMG is almost the same as using Blueprints, but there is additional functionality that we use when we are visually designing our UI.

In this chapter, we'll cover the following topics:

- The Widget Blueprint window
- Setting up an interactive menu
- Commonly used widgets
- Adding widgets to other widgets

So, let's get started.

The Widget Blueprint window

The first thing we need to do is create our own widget by going through the following steps:

1. In the **Content Browser**, navigate to the `ThirdPersonBP\Blueprints` folder.
2. Right-click on the folder, then, at the bottom of the menu, hover over **User Interface** and click on **Widget Blueprint**.

3. Name it `MyWidget`. We now have our **Widget Blueprint** asset, which is represented by a health bar icon, as shown in the following screenshot:

4. Double-click on the **Widget Blueprint** asset and you should see the **Designer** menu for our **Widget Blueprint** asset appear as follows:

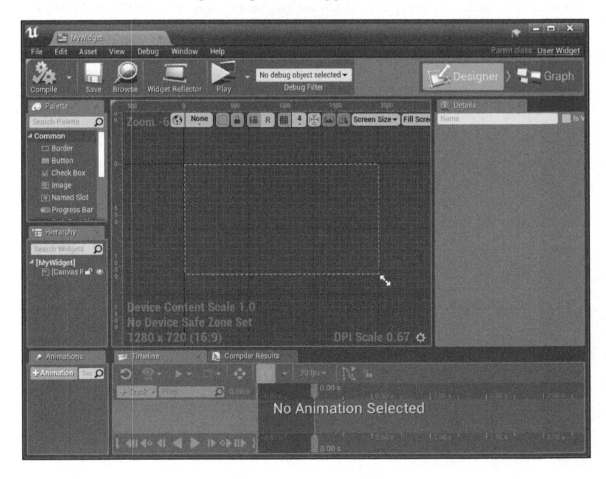

This is where we will add our UI elements—that is, all of the buttons, health bars, and other HUD and menu elements will be created in this **Designer** window.

In the top-right of this window, you will see the **Designer** and **Graph** buttons. If you click on **Graph**, you will see our familiar Blueprint window where we can add variables, functions, and code. We will be using this window very soon, but for now, let's go back to the **Designer** window.

Showing Widget Blueprints in our game

Before we dive into creating and customizing our Widget Blueprints, we first need to display them in our game. We will begin by using our **MyWidget** Blueprint as a HUD.

There are several ways we can add the HUD widget, and there are also a number of places where we can put the code, such as in a custom `PlayerController` class or in a HUD class; however, to keep things simple, we will use our `ThirdPersonCharacter` class, which is in `ThirdPersonBP\Blueprints`. Let's set this up by going through the following steps:

1. Open up the **ThirdPersonCharacter** Blueprint and navigate to **Event Graph**.
2. Right-click on the **Code** window and type `BeginPlay` to place a `BeginPlay` event.
3. Next to it, right-click on the window and type `Create Widget` to place a constructor for the widget classes.
4. Connect the **BeginPlay** output to the widget constructor input.
5. In **Class input**, select **MyWidget** from the drop-down menu.
6. Widgets require a `PlayerController` class as their owner, so, under the **BeginPlay** event, right-click and type `Get Player Controller` to place that node.
7. Connect the **Get Player Controller** output to the **Owning Player** input of the widget constructor.
8. This code will create the widget, but we need to do one more thing to display it. Drag a connection from the **Return Value** output of the widget constructor and type `Add To Viewport` to create a function call, which should automatically connect to the execution output.

The code in our `ThirdPersonCharacter` class should be as follows:

![Blueprint node graph showing Event BeginPlay and Get Player Controller nodes connected to a Create My Widget Widget node with Class set to My Widget, whose Return Value connects to an Add to Viewport node with Target is User Widget.]

Compile, save, and close the **ThirdPersonCharacter** Blueprint and head back to our **My Widget Designer** window. We've set up our widget to display, but right now, there's nothing on it. So let's fix that by going through the following steps:

1. In the upper-left corner of the **Designer** window, you'll see a **Palette** tab, which has a list of available widgets that we can add to our UI. In the **Common** category near the bottom, you will see **Text**. Drag the property into the main **Designer** window.
2. By default, text will display `Text Block`, so let's change that as well. In the right-hand side **Details** tab, under the **Content** category, we will see the **Text** property. Let's change it to `Oh hi Mark!`.
3. Note that this will overlap the widget a bit, so hover over the dot in the bottom-right of the widget's green boundary box and expand it slightly, so that all of the text is inside it. You should now see something similar to the following screenshot in your **Designer** window:

This is all we need for now, so compile the **Widget Blueprint** and save it. Run the game, and we should see our text displayed on screen, as shown in the following screenshot:

Now that we have a widget displayed on the screen, let's set up the foundation for our game's main menu.

Setting up an interactive menu

Since HUDs are not meant to be interactive, we will need a **Widget Blueprint** that we can interact with to try out some of the widget types and widget interactions, such as button presses and text input boxes. A main menu for our *Awesome Game* is perfect for this, so let's create one by going through the following steps:

1. We will need a separate level to act as the main menu. At the top of the main editor window, navigate to **File | New Level**.

2. Select **Default** for the new level. If the editor asks you to save anything, make sure you do so.

3. Once the new level is created, go into the **World Settings** tab on the right-hand side of the editor and, under the **Game Mode** category, set **GameMode Override** to **GameMode**. This class uses a `DefaultPawn` class for our player; this acts more like a spectator camera, which is suitable for our main menu.

4. In the `ThirdPersonBP\Blueprints` folder of the **Content Browser**, right-click and create another **Widget Blueprint** (under **User Interface**); name this one `My Main Menu`.

5. In the top toolbar's main editor window, click on the **Blueprints** button, and then click on **Open Level Blueprint** underneath.

6. This **Blueprint** window is specific to this level, so it's a perfect place to put our main menu creation code. Drag a connection from the **BeginPlay** event and type `Create Widget`, and then set its class to `My Main Menu`.

7. Create a **Get Player Controller** node and hook its output to the **Owning Player** input of the widget creation node.

8. Now drag a connection from the **Return Value** output of the widget creation node and type `Add To Viewport` to create the node.

9. If we left it here, then we would be controlling the camera using the mouse and we wouldn't be able to interact with the menu, so let's add one more node to change that. Drag a connection from the **Add To Viewport's** execution output and type `Set Input Mode`. Then, add a **Set Input Mode UI Only** node. This will allow the mouse to take control of the UI instead of the camera.

10. The **Set Input Mode** node requires two inputs, so connect the **Return Value** output of the widget creation node to the **In Widget to Focus** input, and then connect **Get Player Controller** to the **Player Controller** input of the **Set Input Mode** node.

11. By default, the mouse cursor is hidden, even with the input mode in the UI only. So, drag another connection from the **Get Player Controller** node and type `Show Mouse Cursor` to place a **Set** node for that variable.

12. Check the **Show Mouse Cursor** checkbox in this **Set** node and connect the execution pin to the output of **Set Input Mode** node.

We're done with the **Level Blueprint**, so compile it, and save the level as `Main Menu Map` in the `ThirdPersonBP\Maps` folder.

There was quite a lot to do there, so let's make sure that the code looks OK. I've cleaned it up with reroute nodes (remember that you can double-click on a connecting line to create one), so your code should look something like the following screenshot:

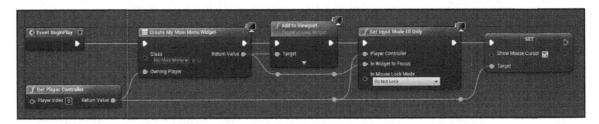

Now, let's move on to the **My Main Menu Widget** Blueprint, as follows:

1. For a quick functional test, let's drag a button from the **Palette** tab on the left side to the main **Designer** window.

2. Hover over the dot on the bottom-right of the green bounding box and expand it to make it larger.

3. We don't need to do anything else at the moment, so compile it and save the **My Main Menu Widget** Blueprint.

Now, when we run our game with the **Main Menu Map** widget open, we will see our **My Main Menu Widget** on the screen as well as our mouse cursor, and we can click on the button.

The button doesn't do anything at the moment, but we will start adding some code after we go over some of the common widgets that we can add to our own blueprint, and learn how to customize them to fit our game's style.

Commonly used widgets

UE4 comes with a variety of common widgets that we can use to create our interfaces. These are provided in the **Palette** tab, which we used for the **Text** and **Button** in our HUD and main menu. You will be able to see a long list of available widgets there, as shown in the following screenshot:

Let's go over some of the common types. Additionally, we will explore several of the properties in the **Details** panel on the right-hand side of the **Designer** window, which are specific to these types of widgets.

The Common section

The following widgets can be found in the **Common** section of the **Palette** tab

Button

Buttons perform Blueprint functions they are pressed. To change how they look, we will go to **Appearance** | **Style**, where we will find options to define the color or texture of the four button states (that is, normal, hovered, pressed, and disabled). Sound effects for hovering over and pressing the button can also be found here.

Checkbox

The checkbox is used for toggling Boolean properties—for example, if the player wanted to invert the *y* axis on their mouse, then you would use one of the following on a settings menu:

- **Style**: You can define custom images and colors for the checkbox here
- **Appearance | Checked State**: This changes the default state of the checkbox

Image

The **Image** widget displays a texture. It can be a simple static image—for example, a background for the menu. It can also be changed during play—for example, an icon for the current weapon that the player is holding. Under this section, you have **Appearance | Brush**, which defines the texture or material that you can use.

> Note that materials must use the UI Material Domain in order to be displayed.

Progress Bar

The **Progress Bar** widget is commonly used for health/stamina bars. These can also be used to show the remaining charge on a weapon. It can also be used for a *use* bar; this is for actions such as unlocking a door or reviving a teammate. We have the following options to set this up:

- **Style**: These properties are used to change the visuals for the background, fill, and marquee
- **Progress | Percent**: This is the default value for the progress bar if it starts at anything other than zero
- **Progress | Bar Fill Type**: This changes the direction in which the progress bar fills
- **Progress | Is Marquee**: This changes the progress bar to display a *loading* style animation

Slider

The **Slider** widget adjusts a float between preset values. It is used for things such as the mouse sensitivity setting or the HUD opacity, as shown in the following list:

- **Appearance | Value**: This is the default value of the slider, which is between zero and one
- **Appearance | Orientation**: This allows you to determine whether this is a horizontal slider or a vertical slider
- **Style**: This changes the visual appearance of the bar and the handle of the slider

Text

The text in a **Text** widget can either be static or it can be changed during play—for example, for displaying the name of the current weapon that the player has equipped. We can adjust the settings using the following sections:

- **Appearance | Font**: This section is used to change the font, size, material, and outline of the text if desired
- **Appearance | Justification**: This is used to change the text's alignment to the left, center, or right
- **Wrapping**: If the text for this box extends outside the boundaries of this widget, then these properties can be used to control if and how the text will wrap on to a new line

The Input section

A little further down the list, you'll see the **Input** section, as shown in the following screenshot:

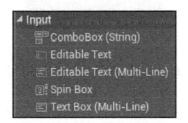

This section deals with widgets that we can directly type into. The main two widgets that we'll want to look at are described in the following sections.

ComboBox

The **ComboBox** widget provides you with a drop-down menu of a list of options for you to select from, as shown in the following list:

- **Content**: If the list is hardcoded, this is where the options for it will be added.
- **Style:** Combo boxes have a lot of style options. Additionally, they also include the option to set every other row to different styles (for example, the **Even Row** and **Odd Row** style properties). The font for the text is also defined here.

Editable Text

There are a few variations of this widget (including **Text Box (Multiline)** and **Editable Text (Multiline)**, but **Editable Text** is the most commonly used one. It can allow the player to set their character name, for example, or it can be used as the input for a chat window. The properties are similar to the **Text** widget, but this one has an additional feature. Under this section, you will find **Appearance | Is Password**; here, the text will display as dots instead of the text that is inputted.

The Primitive and Special Effects sections

The two other sections that you'll want to explore are **Primitive** and **Special Effects**, as shown in the following screenshot:

Here, there are two elements that may be useful to us as visual flair.

Circular Throbber and Throbber

The **Circular Throbber and Throbber** elements can be used as loading icons, and both have options in the **Appearance** section of their properties to adjust the visuals and speed of the icons.

Background Blur

The **Background Blur** will blur everything behind it, including the level. It is commonly used for pause screens and other menus in order to provide a bit of visual flair and to prevent things happening in the level from distracting the user from the menu. Within this section, you can navigate to **Appearance** | **Blur Strength**; here, larger values blur more, but they will also cost more in terms of performance.

Now that we've explored some of the common widgets available to us, let's put some of them to use.

Using widget events

In the same way that events such as **BeginPlay** and **Tick** are available to us in the Blueprint classes, most widgets have specific events that we can use.

In the case of buttons, for example, we will want them to actually do something when they are pressed, and we may want a special functionality for hovering over them as well (for example, to show a preview image on another widget).

Let's set up an example to put this into use:

1. In our **My Main Menu** widget, go to the **Designer** window.
2. Drag a **Button** widget and a **Text** widget from the **Palette** tab onto our widget in the main window, and place the text above the button.
3. In the **Hierarchy** tab underneath the **Palette** tab, right-click on the button, and then click on **Rename**. The names of the widgets here are just for our reference, making our code easier to read. Name the button `Button_ChangeText`, and rename the text widget as `Text_CurrentTime`.
4. At the moment, the **Text** widget is simply decorative and it isn't available to us in the blueprint; however, that can easily be changed. With the **Text** widget selected, you will see that there is an **Is Variable** checkbox in the **Details** tab in the top-right of the window. Check it and you will notice that the widget's name will change to bold in the **Hierarchy** tab.

Our **Designer** window should now look as follows:

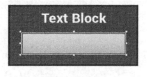

Now it's time to start adding some code. Here, we will need to use one of the button's events, so let's take a look at them. With a widget selected, the list of available events will appear all the way at the bottom of the **Details** tab. You will need to scroll down to see it.

For our button, this is what we will see:

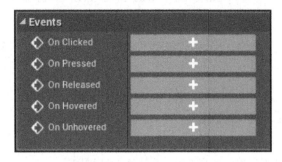

In order to decide which of these events we want to use, let's take a look at how they work:

- **On Clicked**: This is called when the mouse is pressed and released while hovering over the button. This might seem like an obvious event to want, but let's take a look at the next two events, which each have a slightly different behavior that we may want to use.
- **On Pressed**: This is different from **On Clicked**. This is called as soon as the mouse button is pressed down, while **On Clicked** waits for the mouse button to be released.
- **On Released**: This one might appear to be redundant at first, but it is different from **On Clicked**. **On Clicked** is only called when the mouse press and release both happen while the cursor is over the button. With **On Released**, it is called even if the cursor is moved off of the button after being pressed.
- **On Hovered**: This is called when the mouse cursor is over the button.
- **On Unhovered**: This is called when the mouse cursor is no longer over the button.

For our purposes, we will only need to use **On Clicked**. If you press the large green button next to the event, you will be taken to the **Graph** window and our **On Clicked** event will show, as shown in the following screenshot:

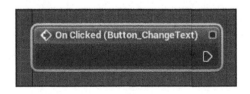

Here, we can also see why the names of our widgets in the **Hierarchy** tab are important. This is because every button's **On Clicked** event will start with **On Clicked**, but it will also show the name of the button that it's attached to.

It's now time for some code. We will want to see some obvious change to the text when we press the button, so let's plug the current game time into it, as follows:

1. In the **My Blueprint** tab on the left-side of the **Graph** window, drag our `Text_CurrentTime` variable out onto the graph and make a **Get** node. This is where the **Is Variable** checkbox comes into play. Note that we would not be able to use the **Text** widget here if the **Is Variable** checkbox was not checked.
2. Drag a connection from the **Text Current Time** node and type `Set Text` to create a **Set Text** node.
3. Connect the **On Clicked** event's output to the **Set Text** node.
4. Right-click below all of this and type `Get Time Seconds`. This node tells us how much time has elapsed since the game started.
5. Drag a connection from the **Get Time Seconds** node and connect it to the **In Text** input of the **Set Text** node. This will automatically create the conversion node between them.

We're done with the code, so let's now compile and save our **My Main Menu Widget**. Our code should look like the following screenshot:

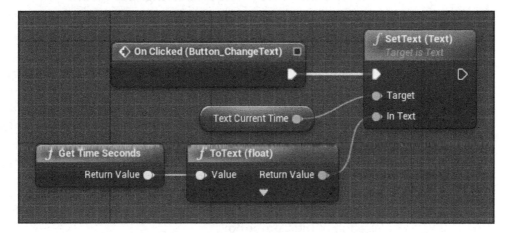

Now let's run the game. Every time we press the button, the **Text** widget should update with the game's current running time, as shown in the following screenshot:

Now that we have an example of a **Widget Event**, let's go back over our list of common widgets and examine which events could be useful for us. Some of the more common ones (aside from **Button**, which we've already covered) include the following:

- **Checkbox**:
    - **On Check State Changed**: This is called when the checkbox is clicked on in order to change it from checked to unchecked and vice versa. Note that this is not called if the mouse button is moved away from the checkbox before being released.
- **Slider**:
    - **On Mouse/Controller Capture Begin**: These events are called when the mouse or controller are pressed.
    - **On Mouse/Controller Capture End**: These events are called when the mouse or controller are released. They can also be called even if the mouse cursor is no longer hovering over the slider.
    - **On Value Changed**: As the slider is moved, this event is called and passes the current value of the slider.
- **ComboBox**:
    - **On Generate Widget**: This is called as a function instead of an event because it needs a widget as a **Return Value**. This is an advanced function, and it is used if you would like to populate the **ComboBox** with custom widgets instead of just having a text list.
    - **On Selection Changed**: This is called when the currently selected index changes. It is not called if the current one is clicked on again; however, be warned that this event is also called when the selection is set directly in code, so make sure that you avoid infinite loops if this event calls a function that directly sets the selection of the **ComboBox**.
    - **On Opening**: This is called when the combo box is clicked on and its list of selections is displayed.

- **Editable Text**:
  - **On Text Changed**: This is called as the player types into the textbox or presses backspace or *Delete*. The event also passes the current text of the textbox with the event.
  - **On Text Committed**: This is called when the player either presses *Enter* or clicks elsewhere on the menu.

Now that we've explored **Widget** events in detail, let's take a look at how we can pass information to our widgets to make them more useful.

Widget set nodes

With our **Get Time Seconds** test, we passed the current game time to a widget, but we found that this wasn't very useful. So what if, for *Awesome Game*, we had a widget on the HUD that let us know how many of our texture spheres were left?

We've finished with the main menu for now, but we'll be coming back to it. Save and close the **My Main Menu Widget**. In the main editor window, go to the **Content Browser's** ThirdPersonBP\Maps folder and double-click on **ThirdPersonExampleMap** to open it. You will need to double-check to make sure that we still have a few of our spheres in the map. If we do not, then go to the ThirdPersonBP\Blueprints folder and drag a few of our **Pickup_MaterialSwitcher** blueprints onto our level. For this test, it won't matter what material is on them, but you can change them if you prefer.

Now for our widget. We'll be using the **MyWidget** class that we previously set up as our HUD for this example:

1. Open the **MyWidget** Blueprint.
2. Place a **Text** widget near the upper-left corner in the **Designer** window. You can also delete the **Oh hi Mark!** widget, if you prefer.
3. With the **Text** widget selected, go to the **Details** tab on the right-side of the window and, under **Appearance | Font**, change **Size** to a larger value, such as 140, to make the text easier to see.
4. Under **Content**, change the Text variable to 0 (zero).
5. At the top of the **Details** tab, check the **Is Variable** checkbox.
6. To the left of the **Is Variable** checkbox, set the name of our widget to Remaining Spheres. Note that this is another place where we can set widget names.

7. In the main **Designer** window, hover over the bottom-right of the **Text** widget and expand the bounding box to cover all of the text. Make it twice as wide as the zero to ensure that two-digit numbers will still be covered.

8. We've now finished with the **Designer** tab, so switch over to the **Graph** tab.

9. We'll be using our own function to update the **Text** widget, so click on the plus sign next to **Functions** in the **My Blueprint** tab on the left. Name this new function Update Remaining Spheres.

10. Right-click on this new function and type Get Game Mode to create the node.

11. Drag a connection from the **Return Value** output of this node, type Cast, and then cast it to **ThirdPersonGameMode**.

12. Drag a connection from the **ThirdPersonGameMode** output of this cast and type Remaining Pickups to get the variable (which we set up in Chapter 2, *Programming Using Blueprints*).

13. Drag a **Get** node for our **Remaining Spheres** variable out into the window.

14. Create a **Set Text** node from the output of the **Remaining Spheres Get** node.

15. Connect the output of the **Remaining Pickups** node to the **In Text** input of the **Set Text** node. This will automatically create the conversion node for it.

16. Connect the execution output of the **Cast** node to the input of the **Set Text** node.

The code for this function should now look as follows:

Now we need to call the following function:

1. In the **Event** tab, locate the **Construct** event; alternatively, right-click and type Construct to create one if it is not there. The **Construct** node acts as a **BeginPlay** type event for the **Widget** classes.

2. Type Update Remaining Spheres to make a call to our function.

Our **Event Graph** tab should look as follows:

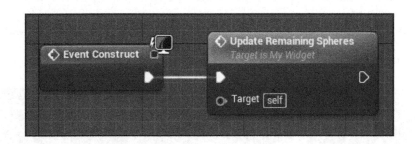

We've finished with the **My Widget** class, so compile it, save it, and then close it.

Now we need to perform some additional steps in our **ThirdPersonCharacter** class:

1. Open up the **ThirdPersonCharacter** Blueprint.
2. We will need a reference to the **My Widget** instance that we created in BeginPlay, so in the **Variables** tab on the left-hand side, press the plus sign.
3. Name this new variable **My Widget Ref**, and in the **Details** tab on the right-side of the window, change **Variable Type** to **MyWidget** (object reference).
4. In the **Event Graph** tab, find the **BeginPlay** event. Place a **Set** node for our **My Widget Ref** variable in between the **Create Widget** node and the **Add to Viewport** node.

The code in our **ThirdPersonCharacter** class should look as follows:

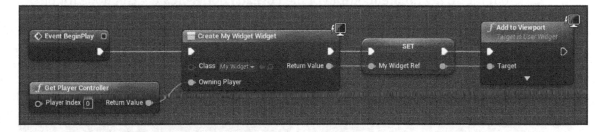

We've finished with this class now, so compile it, save it, and then close it. Next, we'll be working in the **ThirdPersonGameMode** class:

1. Open the **ThirdPersonGameMode** blueprint.
2. In the **Event Graph** tab, locate our **PickupCollected** event. At the end of it, use the **Set Timer by Event** node to create and connect a **Get All Actors of Class** node.

3. Set the **Actor Class** of this node to **Third Person Character**.

4. Connect the **False** output of the **Branch** node to the input of our **Get All Actors of Class** node.

5. Double-click on the connecting line to create reroute nodes if desired.

This section of the code should now look as follows:

Now we can finish the code, as follows:

1. From the **Out Actors** output of the **Get All Actors Of Class** node, create a **ForEachLoop** loop

2. From the **Array Element** output of the **ForEach** node, create a **Get** node for our **My Widget Ref** variable

3. From the **My Widget Ref** variable, call the **Update Remaining Spheres** function

The final code should look as follows:

That's it. You can compile and save the **ThirdPersonGameMode** class. There was a bit more work required for this test, but you should be able to see how everything is now interconnected.

Now, when we run the game, we'll see that the **Text** widget grabs the number of pickups when it is constructed (otherwise, we would see the zero we set it to) and changes when we pick one object up:

Next, we will explore a different way of changing the data of our widgets through **variable binding**.

Variable binding

Widgets can be set to automatically grab data from variables in our widget classes. This is done by binding a property to one of our variables. Let's take a look at how that works:

1. Open the **MyWidget Blueprint**
2. In the **Graph** window, create a variable called `Pickups` and set its variable type to **Text**
3. In the **Update Remaining Spheres** function, delete the **Remaining Spheres GET** node and the **SET Text** function call
4. Create a **SET** node for our new **Pickups** variable and connect it to the **Remaining Pickups Int to Text** conversion and the output of the **ThirdPersonGameMode** cast

The function should now look like the following screenshot:

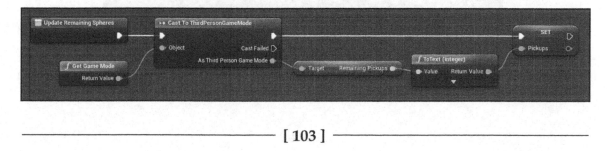

Now that our variable is updating, we just need to bind the **Text** widget's property to it:

1. In the **Designer** window, select the **Text** widget.
2. In the **Details** panel, there is a **Bind** drop-down box next to **Content | Text**. You can select the **Pickups** variable from there.

The **Details** panel will now look like the following screenshot by going through the following steps:

Compile the code and run the game; you'll see it working with the new variable binding.

Another method that we can use involves binding this variable to a function. So, let's do that now:

1. Back in the **Details** panel for our **Text** widget, select the **Create Binding** option in the drop-down list for **Content | Text**
2. This will bring us to the **Graph** window and create a new function for us that returns the text our widget will use
3. Create a **Get** node for our **Pickups** variable and connect it to the **Return Value** output

The function will look like the following screenshot:

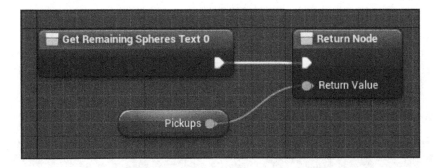

Now, if we compile our code and run the game, the binding will still work.

Binding variables to functions in this way is incredibly useful. Note that it isn't just this text value that we can bind for this widget. If we take a look at the **Details** tab for our **Text** widget (as shown in the following screenshot), we can see that there are three bindings in the **Behavior** section alone (or four if we count the **Tool Tip** property under the **Show Advanced** arrow at the bottom of the section):

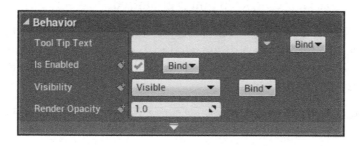

Take the **Is Enabled** property as an example. Say that we had a text input box on a menu of ours, along with an **OK** button. If we didn't want the player to be able to send blank text, we could disable the button until something is inputted in the text box. For this, we could make a binding for the **Is Enabled** property of the button that looks something like the following screenshot:

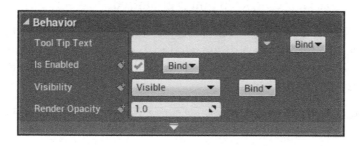

Note that this function gets information from an entirely different widget (that is, an **Editable Text** widget named `Text_Input`) in order to determine whether this button is enabled.

Now that we have a good handle on the inner workings of widgets, let's explore what we can do with widgets as a whole by adding them to other widgets.

Adding widgets to other widgets

Sometimes, our menus and HUDs will become complex. Settings menus, player inventories, and map screens can all have complex designs and layouts. When our widgets reach this point, the **Designer** window can become overly complicated, and the Blueprint window even more so as it tries to keep things organized.

Fortunately, not everything that our widgets use needs to be pieced together from individual buttons, images, and text. If we need to, we can make a smaller widget (such as a chat box, for instance) and add that entire widget to another one (such as our HUD, by pressing *T* to bring up the chat box).

Let's take a look at how to do this in *Awesome Game*. For this example, we're going to set up a list of our pickup spheres and display them on the HUD.

First, let's change how the **Pickup** class works.

Modifying the Pickup class

There are two things we need to do to our `Pickup` class. First, we'll want to add an editable name that we can set on the instances that are placed in the level, so let's do that now:

1. Open our **Base Pickup** class in `ThirdPersonBP\Blueprints`
2. In the **Variables** section on the left-side of the window, press the plus sign button to add a new variable
3. Set the **Variable Type** of this new variable to **String**, and name the **Pickup Name** variable
4. Check the **Instance Editable** box in the **Details** panel so that we can set the name for the pickup instances in the level

Now we need to modify the **Handle Picked Up** function to make sure the UI doesn't add pickups that are in the process of being destroyed. For this, we'll use a Boolean, as follows:

1. Since the **Base Pickup** class sends out its `picked up` function calls before it destroys itself, we'll need a way for our container to know not to add them if they're in the middle of being picked up. For this, add a Boolean variable and call it **Has Been Picked Up**.

2. In the **Handle Picked Up** function, set this new Boolean to **True** at the beginning of the function, as follows:

That's all we need to do to the pickup, so compile, save, and close this class.

Now that the pickup has been modified, we can give the pickups in our level custom names, which will be displayed on the HUD. Let's do that now:

1. Select the pickup spheres in the level one by one. Then, in the **Details** panel on the right-hand side of the editor window, go to the **Default | Pickup Name** property and give each of them a name. For mine, I have set them to the location of the spheres, such as **Top of the Stairs** and **In the Alcove**.

2. Then, save the level.

Now that this part is complete, we can get to work on a new widget; this widget will display the name of each sphere.

Creating the child widget

When we have the list of our pickups on the HUD, we need a widget that is created for each pickup and then added to a container. Things such as kill feeds and inventory menus are also created this way—that is, by having child widgets added to a container. So, let's create our child widget now:

1. In **Content Browser**, right-click on the `ThirdPersonBP\Blueprints` folder and create a new **User Interface | Widget** blueprint. Name it `PickupNameWidget`.

2. In the **Designer** window of our new widget, there is a drop-down option in the top-right of the main **Designer** section. Change the **Fill Screen** option to **Custom**, as demonstrated in the following screenshot:

3. With that changed, you will see that two new options will show up in this area: **Width** and **Height**. Let's set **Width** to 600 and **Height** to 60.

4. Drag a **Text** widget from the **Palette** tab on the left-hand side onto our **Designer** window.

5. Now let's put it in the right place and size. In the **Details** panel on the right-hand side, the first section is called **Slot**. In this section, set **Position X** to 0.0, **Position Y** to 10.0, **Size X** to 600.0, and keep **Size Y** at 40.0. Our properties should now look like the following screenshot:

6. There is one more step here: with our **Text** widget still selected, check the **Is Variable** box at the top of the **Details** panel, and set the name to PickupNameText.

Well, we have finished with the **Designer** window for now. Our widget should look like the following screenshot:

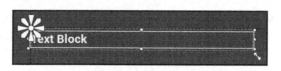

Now, let's switch over to the **Graph** tab. We won't require any code for this widget, but we will need one variable. Let's set this up by going through the following steps:

1. Create a variable in the **My Blueprint** tab on the left-hand side.
2. Name this new variable `PickupName` and set its **Variable Type** to **String**.
3. Check both the **Instance Editable** and **Expose on Spawn** boxes.
4. Switch over to the **Designer** window.
5. With the **Text** widget selected in the main window, navigate to the **Details** panel in the **Content | Text** property. Click on the **Bind** button and set it to our `PickupName` variable.
6. Finally, compile, save, and close this widget.

Now we need a container for these widgets to be added to. Let's create a new widget for this next.

Creating the container widget

The container widget is what the child widgets we just created will be added to. Ours will be a simple vertical list, but other types of containers are also possible, such as horizontal-style containers or grid-style containers, which is useful for inventory screens. So, let's create our container as follows:

1. In **Content Browser**, right-click on the `ThirdPersonBP\Blueprints` folder and create a new **User Interface | Widget** blueprint. Name it `PickupNameContainer`.
2. In this new widget's **Designer** window, change **Fill Screen** to **Custom**, as we did with our previous widget.
3. Set **Width** to 600 and **Height** to 600.
4. For the container itself, we will be using a **Vertical Box**. This is a widget that displays the elements that are added to it arranged vertically, like a list. There are other similar widgets, such as **Horizontal Box**, **Scroll Box**, and **Uniform Grid** panel, which we can use depending on our needs. But, for now, grab a **Vertical Box** from the **Panel** section of the **Palette** tab and drag it onto our main **Designer** window.

5. We need this **Vertical Box** to fill up the entire widget. In the **Details** tab on the right-hand side, let's set both **Position X** and **Position Y** to 0 and both **Size X** and **Size Y** to 600.

6. In the top of the **Details** tab, check the **Is Variable** box and set the name of the **Vertical Box** to `PickupNameBox`.

We've finished with the **Designer** window for now, so let's switch over to the **Graph** window and go through the following steps:

1. We will use a **Custom Event** to handle adding the names, so right-click on the **Event Graph** and make a new **Custom Event**. Name this new event `RefreshPickupNames`.

2. Drag a reference from our **Pickup Name Box** variable onto the graph. Drag a connection from the output and create a **Clear Children** node. Since we'll be updating this **Vertical Box** every time we pick up a sphere, this will prevent the list from having the old widgets as duplicates. From the output of the **Clear Children** node, create a **Get All Actors Of Class** node with **Actor Class** set to **Base Pickup**.

3. From the **Out Actors** array of this node, create a **ForEachLoop** loop. So far, our code should look like the following screenshot:

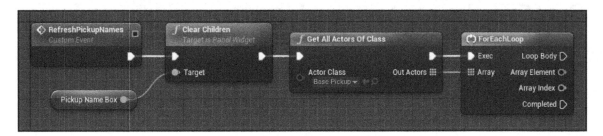

4. From the **Array Element** output of the **ForEach** loop, type `HasBeenPickedUp` to create a **Get** node for that variable.

5. From the **Has Been Picked Up** output, create a **Branch** node.

6. From the **False** output of the **Branch** node, add a **Create Widget** node with **Class** set to **Pickup Name Widget**.

7. When we do this, the **Pickup Name** input should appear, since we set that variable to **Expose on Spawn**. To hook it up, drag a connection from the **Array Element** output of the **ForEachLoop** loop, and type `Pickup Name` to create a **Get** node for that variable. Hook it into the **Pickup Name** input of the **Create Widget** node.

8. Drag another reference to our **Pickup Name Box** variable out onto the graph. From its output, create an **Add Child to Vertical Box** node.

9. Connect the **Return Value** output of **Create Pickup Name Widget** to the **Content** input of the **Add Child** node.

Now we're done with this blueprint, and the code from the **ForEachLoop** loop should look like the following screenshot:

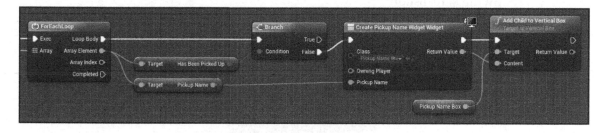

Finally, compile, save, and close this **Widget Blueprint**.

Now for the final steps. We need to add our container to the HUD and hook up its event.

Adding the container to the HUD

Now that our container is created, we need to place it in our HUD and hook it up. We can begin to see how complex we can make our UI, and how flexible it can be. By creating sections of our menus as their own widgets and then adding them to other widgets, we can easily make them reusable and avoid having to recreate them every time we need to place them on a different menu or HUD.

For instance, if we had a different HUD for *Deathmatch* and for *Capture the Flag*, we could create a widget for each game mode, but still be able to use separate elements, such as a kill feed and a player health bar, without having to recreate them for each HUD widget

So, let's add our pickup list container to our HUD by going through the following steps:

1. Open our **MyWidget** class.

2. In the **Designer** window, go into the **Palette** tab on the left-hand side. At the bottom of this list will be a **User Created** category. All of our custom widgets will show up here, and can be added to any other widget as we would with buttons, so let's start here. Drag a **Pickup Name Container** widget out onto the **Designer** window.

3. For this one, we'll place it near the top-right corner, so drag it there.

4. You'll notice a star-like icon appear when we have a widget selected. This is called the anchor, and determines where a widget gets its relative position. Since this changes depending on the screen resolution, we want to make sure that we anchor widgets to the correct location. For this container, it will be in the upper-right corner, so in the **Details** tab on the right-hand side, navigate to the **Slot** category (at the top). In the **Anchors** drop-down menu, select the top-right corner option. We'll see the anchor move to the top-right corner, as shown in the following screenshot:

User-created widgets are automatically set to **Is Variable**, so we've now finished with the **Designer** window. Switch over to **Event Graph** and let's hook up the code:

1. In the **My Blueprint** tab on the left, double-click on our **Update Remaining Spheres** function to open it
2. At the end of this function, drag a reference from our **Pickup Name Container** variable onto the graph
3. From its output, create a call to our **Refresh Pickup Names** function

That's all we need to do. The code should now look like the following screenshot:

You can compile and save this Widget Blueprint.

Now we're finally ready to see it in action. Click on the **Play** button to go into the game, and we'll see the list of pickups appear in the container on the HUD, as shown in the following screenshot:

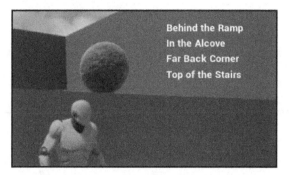

We will also see the list update itself when we pick one up!

Summary

We've gone through a lot in this chapter. We've learned how to create widgets, how to set them up as menus and HUDs, and how to make them interactive. We've gone over some of the commonly used widget types and used them to create our own menu and HUD. We've also demonstrated some of the more advanced uses of widgets, such as adding widgets to other widgets.

There are many other features of widgets that you should consider exploring, such as animations and creating custom materials to use for health bars and more. For more information about this, you can refer to Epic's documentation for widgets at https://docs. unrealengine.com/en-us/Engine/UMG/UserGuide.

In the next chapter, we will be covering the animation system for our characters so that we can change the way they animate. Let's keep going!

Animation Blueprints

5

So far, we've covered a lot of the major systems available to us for making our projects in UE4. Using Blueprints and C++ to program takes us most of the way towards completing a project, and UMG gives us one of the final pieces of the puzzle. In this chapter, we will be covering the Animation Blueprint system, which will let us create more dynamic characters.

Animation used to be straightforward, but it was difficult to create complex systems. With UE4, we have the incredibly powerful Animation Blueprint system available to us, which we can use to create complicated animation sequences for action or fighter games for example.

If we don't need anything too complex, simple adjustments and additions to the Animation Blueprints that come with the project templates will cover anything we need. For the Third-Person Template that we've been using, we'll notice that the idle, run, and jumping and landing animations for our character are already set up by default.

The following topics will be covered in this chapter:

- Creating the attachment
- Creating sockets on Skeletal Meshes
- Spawning and attaching actors
- Modifying the Animation Blueprint

In addition to our characters, Animation Blueprints can be used with weapons and objects in the world to bring more life to our project.

For our Awesome Game project, let's take a look at how we can add on to the existing animations by adding a weapon.

Creating the attachment

Before we start creating the weapon Blueprint, we'll need a suitable mesh for it. By default, the **Third Person** template does not include one, but, if you'll remember from Chapter 1, *Introduction to Unreal Engine 4*, we can import assets from other templates if we find that we need them. In this case we do, so let's grab what we need:

1. In the **Content Browser**, click the **Add New** button and select **Add Feature** or **Content Pack** at the top
2. In the menu that comes up, we should already be in the **Blueprint Feature** tab, so select **First Person** and then click the green **Add to Project** button at the bottom-right

Once that's done, we'll have what we need. If we go into the **Content Browser** and head into the FirstPerson\FPWeapon\Mesh folder, we'll see an asset called SK_FPGun, which is the Skeletal Mesh we will use to create our weapon:

Now that we have the asset we need, let's create the weapon Blueprint:

1. Create a new **Blueprint** class in the ThirdPersonBP\Blueprints folder
2. Select **Actor** as its parent class, and name it TestWeapon
3. Open the new **Blueprint** class and go to its **Viewport** tab
4. Back out in the **Content Browser**, go to the FirstPerson\FPWeapon\Mesh folder and select the **SK_FPGun** asset
5. In our **TestWeapon Blueprint**, click on **Add Component** in the top-left and select **Skeletal Mesh** (it should say **SK_FPGun** after it)
6. This is all we need to do in the weapon class for now, so compile, save, and close this Blueprint

Now we need to attach the weapon to the player. The first step in this process is to create a Socket.

Creating sockets on Skeletal Meshes

Sockets are simply transforms that keep their location relative to a bone in a Skeletal Mesh. We use these to give the player a choice of hats to wear on their character, to spawn particle effects on the player's feet as they run, or, more commonly, to have a character hold different weapons.

Sockets are created in the skeleton of the Skeletal Mesh, so let's track down that asset now:

1. In the `ThirdPersonBP\Blueprints` folder, open the `ThirdPersonCharacter` Blueprint file.
2. In the **Components** list, select the **Mesh** component.
3. In the **Details** panel on the right, take a look at the **Mesh | Skeletal Mesh** property. You'll see that it references a **Skeletal Mesh** asset called `SK_Mannequin`. This is the skeletal mesh that our character uses.
4. Click on the magnifying glass button in this property and the **Content Browser** will go to that asset's location and select it for us. We'll see that it's in the `Mannequin\Character\Mesh` folder.
5. Double-click the `SK_Mannequin` asset to open it. We'll see the **Mesh** for our character in the A-pose.
6. For the socket, we won't be using this **Mesh** window. Instead, we'll be looking at the **Skeleton**. In the upper right hand corner, we'll see buttons that take us to windows for different aspects of the **Skeletal Mesh**, such as the Physics setup, but for now click on the **Skeleton** button:

7. Here we'll also see our character in the A-pose, and we'll also see a long list of bones that make up our character's Skeleton. Follow the tree until you find **hand_r** and select it (that entire portion of the tree will have the **_r** suffix to make it easier to follow):

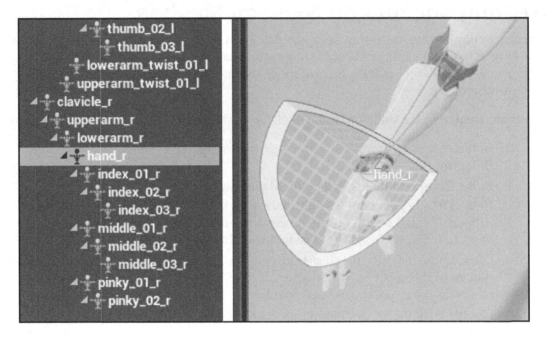

This is the bone we'll be creating the Socket for, which we'll use to attach the weapon. Now let's create the socket.

8. Right-click on the **hand_r** bone in the left panel and click **Add Socket**. It will appear as a child of the **hand_r** bone in the bones list, and as a diamond shape in the 3D Viewport.

9. Instead of blindly spawning the attachment in code and having to adjust its position by trial and error, we can preview it right here in the **Skeleton** window. Let's set up that preview **Mesh** now.

10. Select the **hand_rSocket** that we created in the bone list on the left.

11. Right-click the **hand_rSocket** and hover over **Add Preview Asset**.

12. Scroll down or type **SK_FPGun** in the search box to find our gun asset and select it. We'll see that the preview mesh appears, but it is in the wrong location and rotation:

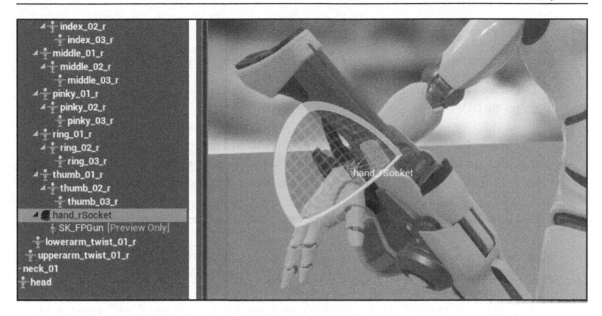

13. We can adjust it using the transform gizmo in the 3D Viewport as well as fine tune it using the Relative properties in **Details | Socket Parameters** on the right of the window. It doesn't need to be perfect for now. These are the values I came up with:

Our socket setup is complete, so press the **Save** button in the upper left-hand corner in this **Skeleton** window so we don't lose our progress.

Now that our Socket is set up, we need to spawn and attach our weapon class to the player when the game starts up. Let's do that now.

Spawning and attaching Actors

There are two steps to this process, and we'll be doing both in our character Blueprint:

1. Go into the **Content Browser's** `ThirdPersonBP\Blueprints` folder and open up our `ThirdPersonCharacter` Blueprint.

2. At the end of our **BeginPlay** Event where we create the HUD widget, drag a connection from the **Add to Viewport** node and create a **Spawn Actor** from **Class** node. This is used to create an instance of a Blueprint in the world.

3. Set this node's **Class** input to **TestWeapon** using the drop-down list.

4. Spawn nodes need the **Spawn Transform** to be connected to something, so right-click and create a **Get Actor Transform** node and connect it to the **Spawn Transform** input.

5. Now we need to store a reference to this spawned Actor that we can use later. In the **My Blueprint** tab on the left, create a new variable and set its **Variable Type** to **TestWeapon**, and its name to `MyWeapon`.

6. Create a **Set** node for this variable connected to the outputs of the **Spawn** node.

7. That's all we need to do to spawn the weapon, so now let's attach it.

8. Drag a connection from the **Spawn** node's output and create an **Attach To Component** node.

9. Connect the **Return Value** of the **Spawn** node to the **Target** input of the **Attach** node.

10. Drag a reference to our **Mesh** component from the **Components** tab in the upper left-hand corner and connect it to the **Parent** input of the **Attach** node.

11. Set the **Socket Name** of the **Attach** node to our Socket's name, which, by default, should be **hand_rSocket**.

12. For the **Location**, **Rotation**, and **Scale Rule**, set all of them to **Snap to Target**. This will make sure the relative location and rotation we set up for the Socket will be used.

13. Compile and save this **ThirdPersonCharacter** Blueprint.

Now the code at the end of our **BeginPlay** Event should look like this:

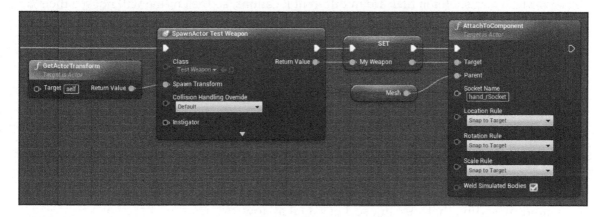

Now if we run our game we'll see our character running around with the **TestWeapon**:

Right now it looks odd, but next we'll start working in the Animation Blueprint to customize how all of our animations fit together.

Animation retargeting

Now, we'll make our animation setup look more natural. To do this, we're going to need to use one of the animations from the Animation Starter Pack. If you do not have this installed, please refer to the *Adding Marketplace Items To Your Project* section of Chapter 1, *Introduction to Unreal Engine 4*.

But there's a problem. Even though the animations are built around the same model, the Skeletal Mesh and skeleton files are in different locations, so the engine will not see them as compatible, as they won't work on our character's model by default.

This is going to be a common problem for anyone relying on third-party animations for their project, so let's talk about how to fix this using Animation Retargeting.

First, let's decide which animation we need. We're not going to want everything from the Animation Starter Pack. For running around carrying a rifle, in the `AnimStarterPack` folder we will want the `Idle_Rifle_Hip` animation file.

To retarget this animation, we're going to need to modify both the origin and target skeletons so the animation knows which bones are which when going from the original skeleton to the new one. Luckily for us, Epic has simplified this process with a default humanoid rig setting that we can use. Let's do that now.

Setting up the source Skeleton

There are a few simple steps to this process, made easier with Epic's humanoid rig preset:

1. For the origin skeleton in the Animation Starter Pack, go into the `AnimStarterPack\UE4_Mannequin\Mesh` folder and open the `UE4_Mannequin_Skeleton` file.
2. Press the **Retarget Manager** button in the top toolbar.
3. In the **Set up Rig** section on the left, choose the **Select Humanoid Rig** option in the Select **Rig** drop-down list here:

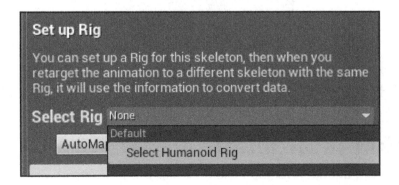

When this is selected, you will see a long list of bones come up that have automatically been assigned to their proper targets:

If we were working with a custom Skeleton, these would need to be adjusted, but it will try to fill in these options as best it can for those. With Epic's rig, all of the options are filled in correctly, so we're done with this Skeleton file.

Save and close this file. Now we'll set up the target Skeleton.

Setting up the target Skeleton

Setting up this skeleton uses the same process:

1. Go to the `Mannequin\Character\Mesh` folder and open the `UE4_Mannequin_Skeleton` file
2. Repeating the same process, press the **Retarget Manager** button and choose the **Select Humanoid Rig** option in the Select **Rig** drop-down list
3. Save and close this file

Now for the animation retargeting.

Retarget the animation

Now that both Skeletons have been set up, we can retarget the animation:

1. In the `AnimStarterPack` folder, right-click the `Idle_Rifle_Hip` animation and select **Retarget Anim Assets | Duplicate Anim Assets and Retarget**.
2. A **Select Skeleton** window will come up. There are two options we'll need to set here. The first is the target skeleton. Compatible Skeletons will be listed on the left-hand side, so click on our **UE4_Mannequin_Skeleton**.

3. By default, the new file will end up in the `root Content` folder, which we don't want. Press the **Change** button in the bottom right-hand corner, and select the `Mannequin\Animations` folder as the new destination and hit **OK**.

Our **Select Skeleton** window should look like this now:

Press the **Retarget** button and the animation will be duplicated to the `Mannequin\Animations` folder and be ready to use with our **ThirdPersonCharacter**.

There's just one final step before we implement this animation: we're going to add a control to our character so it knows when we want to use the animation.

Adding a weapon Equip control

We've done this before in `Chapter 2`, *Programming Using Blueprints*, when we added a Sprint control to our character, so this should be familiar. This time we're going to add an **Equip** control:

1. In the main editor window, go to **Edit | Project Settings**.
2. In the **Engine** section, click on the **Input** option.

3. We need to add an Action Mapping. Click the + button next to Action Mappings. Name this new one **Equip**, and assign it the **Mouse Wheel Axis** key. This will fire when the mouse wheel is scrolled up or down.

The new Action Mapping should look like this:

Now we need to add some code to implement this event:

1. Go to the `ThirdPersonBP\Blueprints` folder and open the `ThirdPersonCharacter` file.
2. In the **Event Graph**, right-click and add our **Equip InputAction**.
3. In the **My Blueprint** tab on the left, create a new Boolean variable and name it `bWeaponEquipped`.
4. From the **Pressed** output of the **Equip** event, create a Set node for the **bWeaponEquipped** variable.
5. Create a **Get** node for the **bWeaponEquipped** variable, and hook it into a **NOT** node, then hook that into the input of the variable's **Set** node.

The new code in our **ThirdPersonCharacter** Blueprint should look like this:

That's all we need to do here, so let's compile and save this Blueprint. And now, finally, we can work in the Animation Blueprint.

Modifying the Animation Blueprint

An Animation Blueprint works much the same as our other Blueprints. Just as a Widget Blueprint has a **Designer** window, an Animation Blueprint has an **AnimGraph** where we control the flow of animations using variables defined in that Animation Blueprint.

Let's take a look at the one our character uses to get an idea of how it's set up. In the `Mannequin\Animations` folder, open up the `ThirdPerson_AnimBP` file.

When the file opens, the main window might be showing one of the smaller graphs. So, double-click on **Event Graph** in the **My Blueprint** tab on the left and take a look. We'll find two things of interest:

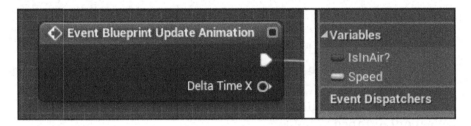

The first is the main event that is used in Animation Blueprints: **Blueprint Update Animation**. This is called every frame, like **Tick** in other Blueprint files. We can see hooked up to this event are two sets for two variables, **IsInAir** and **Speed**.

These variables are used by the animation state system to determine what animations to play. Let's take a look at how each of these is used.

First, we'll take a look at **IsInAir** by learning how the **AnimGraph** works.

The AnimGraph

Below the **Event Graph**, in the My Blueprint tab on the right, there will be an **AnimGraph**. Double-click on it to open it in the main window. We'll see two nodes connected to each other:

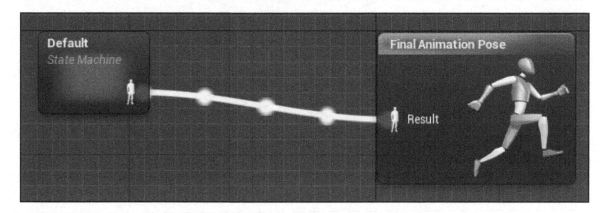

The one on the right, **Final Animation Pose**, is what will be applied to the character. Since this final animation can depend on a lot of different factors, we use a **State Machine** to determine this final animation. For this Animation Blueprint, the state machine is named **Default**.

If we double-click on this **Default** node, we can see this **State Machine** in action:

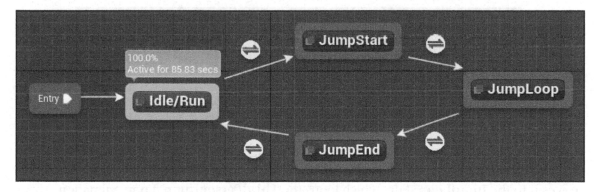

We can see the **Entry** point that all **State Machines** will have. It's connected to an **Idle/Run** state node that is currently running. We can see this with the character preview in the upper left-hand corner of this window.

There are four states in this window, connected by arrows with a circular white icon. Those lines with the icons are called Rules, and they determine when the **State Machine** can enter the state it's connected to.

Let's take a look at how this works. From the **Idle/Run** State there is a Rule connecting it to the **JumpStart** state at the top. Double-clicking on the Rule icon connecting these two states will allow us to see how it works:

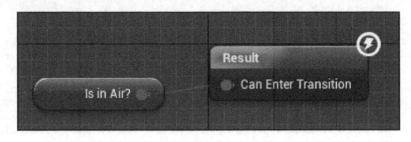

And here we see our **Is In Air** variable. Rules take a Boolean as their input, and when it is **True**, the conditions of the Rule have been satisfied and the **State Machine** will move into the state it's connected to, in this case **JumpStart**.

If we go back to the **Default** window and double-click on **JumpStart**, we'll see it simply plays an animation while in this state:

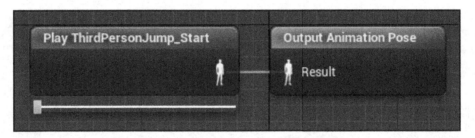

Continuing down the line of the **Default** window, the Rule connecting **JumpStart** to **JumpLoop** simply waits until the **JumpStart** animation is almost finished playing, then moves into the **JumpLoop** state, which loops the **ThirdPersonJump_Loop** animation.

Going back in the other direction toward the bottom of the **Default** window, the Rule connecting **JumpLoop** to **JumpEnd** checks if **Is In Air** is no longer **True**. This moves us into the **JumpEnd** state, which plays the landing animation, and, when that's almost finished, the Rule connecting it back to the **Idle/Run** state moves us back there.

There's a simple way to see this in action. On the bottom right-hand side of the window, we'll see an **Anim Preview Editor** tab that lists our variables:

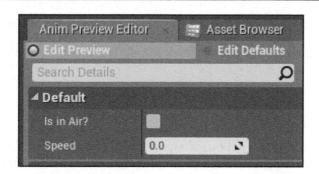

We can change these to preview what will happen to our **State Machine**. Check the **Is In Air** box and we'll see the current state change to **JumpStart** and then to **JumpLoop** and stay there. If we uncheck it again the current state will change to **JumpEnd** and then back to **Idle/Run**.

Knowing all of this, we can easily create our own states and rules to add. Let's say our character could swim. We'd want a state that played swimming specific animations. To do that, we'd drag a connection off of the edge of the **Idle/Run** state and select **State** from the menu that comes up.

Note that when we do this, the Rule connecting them is automatically created. It's a one-way connection by default, so, if we wanted to go back to the **Idle/Run** state after the player got out of the water, we would drag a connection from our **Swimming** state back to the **Idle/Run** state to create the rule going back to **Idle/Run**.

The state setup would look something like this:

Now we can start to see how complex we can make our animation system.

Let's delete this **Swimming** state and go back to take a look at our weapon **equip** animation.

Modifying an Animation state

The first thing we need to do to get our weapon animations working is to grab the **bWeaponEquipped** variable that we set up in our **ThirdPersonCharacter**. We can do this in the **Event Graph** of the Animation Blueprint:

1. Open the **Event Graph** of the ThirdPerson_AnimBP file that we've been looking at.
2. In the **My Blueprint** tab on the lower left, create a new Boolean variable and call it **bWeaponEquipped**.
3. In the main **Blueprint** window, drag a connection from the **Try Get Pawn Owner** node near the beginning (it will have blue connections) and create a Cast to **ThirdPersonCharacter** node all the way at the end.
4. Connect the output of the **Set Speed** node to this **Cast**.
5. From the **As Third Person Character** output of the **Cast**, create a **Get Weapon Equipped** node.
6. From the output of this **Get**, create a **Set** node for the Animation Blueprint's bWeaponEquipped variable.
7. Connect the execution output of the **Cast** to the input of the **Set**.

The code at the end of the **Event Graph** should look like this now:

With that done, we need to modify the **Idle/Run** state. In the **My Blueprint** tab on the left, open the **AnimGraph**, then double-click the **Idle/Run** node to open it up.

Here, we'll see our **Speed** variable, which is plugged into a Blendspace. Blendspaces switch between two or more animations depending on the value of the float that is plugged into them. In this case, as **Speed** increases, the Blendspace switches from an idle to a walking animation, and then from a walking to a running animation as speed increases further.

It's here in this **Idle/Run** state that we'll add our **Idle_Rifle_Hip** animation. One problem we'll immediately notice is that the rifle animation is an idle. If we switched straight to it, our character would be moving around without the legs moving, which would look weird. To get around this, we can use a different type of blend, a layered blend per bone, to only use the upper half of the rifle animation while keeping the lower half of the idle and run animations.

Let's set this up:

1. From the output of the **ThirdPerson_IdleRun_2D Blendspace**, create a Layered Blend Per Bone node.
2. Connect the output of this node to the Output **Animation Pose** node.
3. This blend node needs to know what bone in our skeleton to use as the dividing point. In our case, we'll want to use **spine_01**, which divides the upper and lower halves. With the Layered Blend node selected, go into the **Details** panel on the right and into the **Config** | **Layer Setup** | **0** | **Branch Filters** property.
4. Press the + sign on the **Branch Filters** property, which will create a struct under it.
5. In this **struct**, set the **Bone Name** to **spine_01**. The properties should now look like this:

6. Back in the main window, right-click and create a play **Idle_Rifle_Hip** node, and connect it to the **Blend Poses 0** input of the **Layered Blend** node.
7. Now this Layered Blend needs a blend weight to decide when to blend in the **Idle_Rifle_Hip** animation. Right-click and create a **Get** node for our **bWeaponEquipped** variable, and connect it to the **Blend Weights 0** input of the **Layered Blend** node. This will automatically create the conversion node.

The **Idle/Run** state should now look like this:

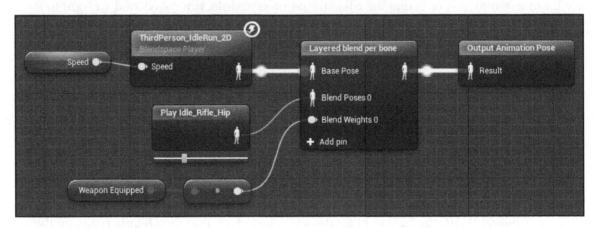

That's all we need to do; so, compile and save this file. Before we close it, we can toggle the **bWeaponEquipped** variable on the right-hand side's **Anim Preview Editor** tab to see our animation working.

There are two other small things we need to do before we're done. By default, our weapon is unequipped, but it is visible in-game. Let's change that:

1. Open the **TestWeapon** Blueprint file
2. Press **Class Defaults** in the top toolbar to show those properties in the **Details** tab on the right
3. Under **Rendering**, check the **Actor Hidden In Game box**
4. Compile, save, and close this Blueprint

Now when we equip the weapon, we want it to show. For that, we'll make a small addition to our **ThirdPersonCharacter** Blueprint:

1. Open the **ThirdPersonCharacter** Blueprint
2. Find the **InputAction Equip** event we created earlier
3. Create a **Get** node for the **MyWeapon** variable we created earlier
4. From that node, create a **Set Actor Hidden In Game** node
5. From the output of the **Set Weapon Equipped** node, create a **NOT** node, then connect its output to the **New Hidden** input of the **Set Actor Hidden** node

The **Equip** event should look like this now:

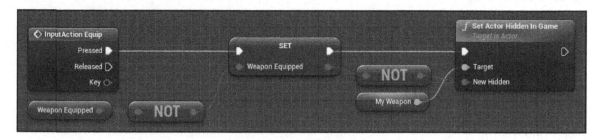

Compile, save, and close the **ThirdPersonCharacter** Blueprint.

Now when we run our game, the weapon should be invisible by default, but when we scroll the mouse wheel it will appear and our character will have the proper animation. When we run, we'll see that the legs work properly while the weapon is being held as well:

It looks a bit odd being instantaneous, though. If we wanted a more smooth transition, instead of having a simple Boolean for the bWeaponEquipped variable in our ThirdPersonCharacter, we could add a float that slowly increased from 0 to 1 and vice versa through the Tick event when the bWeaponEquipped variable changed. In the Animation Blueprint we could grab that float and plug it into the Layered Blend node instead of the Boolean.

Why not give it a try?

Summary

We've taken a pretty good look at Animation Blueprints and how to use them to make our character more dynamic. Through states and rules, we've seen how we can transition from different animation states to reflect the character's interaction with the world, and, by examining a state, we've seen how to further modify them to take other factors into account such as holding a weapon.

In the next chapter, we will look at the Blackboard system to start creating some AI that we can interact with.

6
AI with Behavior Tree and Blackboard

In the last chapter, we covered the Animation Blueprint system, which we can use to create robust systems for our characters and other animated objects. In this chapter, we will take a look at the behavior tree and blackboard systems that we can use to create complex AI for our enemies and other computer controlled characters.

In the past, creating AI with Unreal Engine involved a lot of complex code. Even when using state machines, the code was often difficult to keep organized, and even harder to debug. With Unreal Engine 4, we have an alternative in the behavior tree system, which lets us easily set up and modify AI behavior, as well as see the tree in action in real time to make debugging easier.

The following topics will be covered in this chapter:

- Creating a simple AI
- Behavior Trees
- Setting up a Blackboard
- Using sequences, selectors, tasks, decorators, and services

To start, we're going to create a simple AI that we can use as the base for our behavior tree.

Creating a simple AI

Just like our player-controlled character, an AI controlled character needs both a Pawn and a Controller. While we can use the same Pawn we've been using for our player, let's create custom ones so that we can define some enemy-specific behavior for it.

Creating the Pawn as a separate class is also useful if we want to drastically alter how the Pawn looks; for example, if we wanted to create a spider enemy.

Let's create the custom Pawn now.

Creating a Pawn for the enemy

Creating the Pawn for our enemy is simple, since we have Epic's base classes to extend from, which has most of the functionality we need:

1. In the **Content Browser**, right-click in the `ThirdPersonBP\Blueprints` folder and select the `Blueprint` class.
2. Select **Character** as the parent class, and name this new class `EnemyCharacter`.
3. Open up this new blueprint.
4. By default, this new **Character** will not have a mesh, so let's give it the same one that our player has. With our **EnemyCharacter** blueprint still open, navigate to the `Mannequin\Character\Mesh` folder and select **SK_Mannequin**.
5. Back in **EnemyCharacter**, select its **Mesh** component and then, in the **Details** panel on the right-hand side, click the left arrow button in its **Mesh | Skeletal Mesh** property to assign it. You can also drag the **SK_Mannequin** asset directly on to this property to assign it that way.
6. You can see that the mesh isn't covered by the capsule collision, and is rotated the wrong way. (The light blue **ArrowComponent** shows the forward direction.) Let's fix this quickly. In the **Mesh** component's **Transform** properties, set **Location | Z** to **-97** and its **Rotation | Z** to **270**.
7. The last thing we need to do is make it animate. From the previous chapter, we know that this is done in Animation Blueprints, so let's assign one to this class. For now, it's fine to reuse the same one that our player is using, although we will not have the armed animation functionality that our player has. Go into the `Mannequin\Animations` folder and select the **ThirdPerson_AnimBP** asset; then, back in our `EnemyCharacter` class' **Mesh** component, click the left arrow next to the **Animation | AnimClass** property.

That's all we need to do to create our enemy's Pawn, so, let's compile, save, and close this file.

Now, let's create the controller for this Pawn.

Creating a controller for the enemy Pawn

Next, we need to create the controller for our enemy, which acts as the brain for the Pawn body:

1. In the `ThirdPersonBP\Blueprints` folder, right-click and create a new **Blueprint** class. In the **Search** box for the **Pick Parent** class dialogue, type `AIController` and select that class as the parent.
2. Name this new class `EnemyController` and open it up.

For this simple AI test, we're going to run a repeating event that makes this enemy run to a random location, wait a few seconds, then run to another random location. The first step for this is the code in our `EnemyController` class:

1. In the **Event Graph** of our `EnemyController` class, right-click and create a new **Custom Event** node, and name it `MoveToRandomLocation`.
2. Below this, create a **Get Controlled Pawn** node.
3. From this, we'll want to create two nodes. The first is an **Is Valid** node (the question mark one, not the pure function one with the **f** icon). The second is a **Get Actor Location** node below the **Is Valid** one.
4. Connect the **MoveToRandomLocation** node's output to the **Is Valid** node.
5. From the **Get Actor Location** node, create a **Get Random Reachable Point In Radius** node. This will find a location that this Pawn can actually reach, so we don't have it trying to run through a wall or anything like that.
6. From the **Random Location** output of this node, create a **Move To Location** or **Actor** node. As you're typing this in the function search, you may notice that two other options come up, **Move to Location** and **Simple Move to Location**. The reason why we specifically want the **Move To Location** or **Actor** node is that it is a latent function (discussed in `Chapter 2`, *Programming Using Blueprints*) that provides us with outputs that only fire when the task is complete. This way, we will not interrupt the AI in the middle of a move with a new move, if it's taking longer to complete.
7. Connect the **Is Valid** output of the **Is Valid** node to the execution pin of the **Move To Location** or **Actor** node.

Our code should look like this so far:

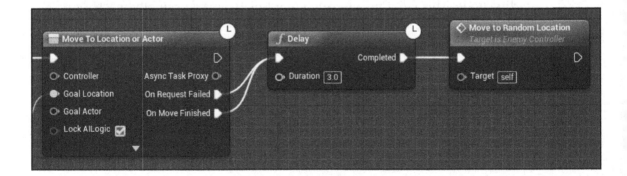

8. From this **Move To Location** or **Actor** node, create a **Delay** node and set it's **Duration** to **3** seconds. Connect both the **On Request Failed** and **On Move Finished** outputs of the **Move** node to it, but do not connect the normal execution output.

9. From the **Delay** node, create a call back to our **Move To Random Location** event. Normally, this would create an infinite loop crash, but the latent functions in this event prevent that from happening. The end of this code block should look like this:

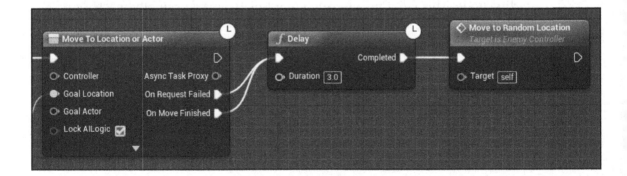

10. There's one final step for this class. From the **BeginPlay** event, create a call to our **Move To Random Location** event to start the loop. This will end up looking like the following screenshot:

Compile, save, and close the previous blueprint. Now, we need to tell our **EnemyCharacter** to use this class as its brain.

1. Open the **EnemyCharacter** asset.
2. Click **Class Defaults** in the top toolbar.
3. In the **Pawn** section, there will be two options at the bottom that we'll want to look at. The first is at the bottom, **AI Controller Class.** This tells the Pawn what class to use as its brain when it is being controlled by an **AIController**. Click the drop-down box and select our **EnemyController** class.
4. The second property, **Auto Possess AI**, is right above that.This determines when the controller is automatically created and assigned to the Pawn. This can either be disabled, set to **Placed In World**, **Spawned**, or both **Placed In World or Spawned**. These options can be useful if we want to have different types of AI that use the same Pawn, and we need to manually spawn and assign a controller. For now, the **Placed In World** default option is all that we need.

Those properties should look like this:

Compile, save, and close this file.

Now, for our enemy to be able to navigate our level, we need to add a Navigation Mesh (Nav Mesh).

Adding a Nav Mesh

We're now done with the code part of this simple AI; but, if we placed it in the level as it is, it wouldn't move. We need to add a Nav Mesh to our level so that the AI knows which parts of the level are navigable:

1. In the main editor window, make sure that our **ThirdPersonExampleMap** is open.
2. In the **Modes** panel in the top-left, make sure that the **Place** button is selected (the first button, which looks like a cube with a few spheres near it).
3. In the **Search Classes** box below that button, type `Nav Mesh` to bring up the **Nav Mesh Bounds Volume** class. Drag one of these out into the level onto the floor.
4. By default, you won't see anything change except the cube of this new actor. We want to see the Nav Mesh so that we can ensure that it covers everything. There are two ways to do this. The first is simply by clicking in the 3D Viewport and pressing *P*. This is the shortcut to show navigation paths. The other way, which we talked about in `Chapter 1`, *Introduction to Unreal Engine 4*, is by clicking on **Show** at the top of the 3D Viewport and checking the navigation box.
5. Now, a green square should show up on the floor where our **Nav Mesh Bounds Volume** is. If not, it may not be overlapping the floor. In any case, this box is too small to be effective for our AI, so we need to scale it up using the transform widget (press *R* as a shortcut for scale). Adjust it in all three directions to make sure it covers the entire floor of the level as well as the stairs and platform above.

The level should look like this now, with the Nav Mesh showing:

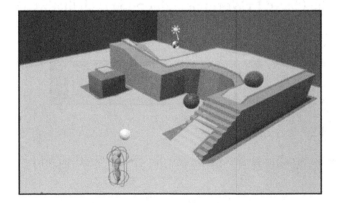

Now that we have the Nav Mesh, we can add the **EnemyCharacter** to the level. Go to the `ThirdPersonBP\Blueprints` folder and drag an **EnemyCharacter** out into the level.

That's all we need to do for our simple AI. Save and run the level and we'll see our AI running around! It is shown as follows:

From this simple test, we can see that AI code can easily become very complicated and difficult to modify without extensive planning or frequent modifications to the existing code. AI code can quickly become unwieldy and prone to bugs.

Luckily, Unreal Engine 4 has a system available to us to make it a lot easier to create, modify, and debug our AI. Let's take a look at Behavior Trees and Blackboard.

Behavior Trees

Behavior Trees act as flowcharts to determine the actions of an AI. Much like the Animation Blueprint, we can use external variables to determine which paths the Behavior Tree takes.

To see this in action, let's create our own Behavior Tree and replace the simple code we've created for our AI with it.

Creating and running a Behavior Tree

Behavior Trees are created like most other assets, so let's head into the **Content Browser**:

1. Go to the `ThirdPersonBP\Blueprints` folder.
2. Right-click, and, under the **Artificial Intelligence** section, select **Behavior Tree**.
3. Name it `EnemyBehavior`.
4. Before we start using this asset, let's set up our **EnemyController** to use it. Open the **EnemyController** blueprint.

5. Delete all of the code from the **Event Graph** except for the **BeginPlay** event.
6. From the **BeginPlay** event, create a **Run Behavior Tree** node.
7. In its **BTAsset** property, select our **EnemyBehavior** asset in the drop-down list.

The code should now look like this:

That's all we need to do in this class, so compile, save, and close it.

That will get our enemy using the Behavior Tree we've created; so, now let's open that asset up and take a look.

Setting up a simple Behavior Tree

If we open up the **EnemyBehavior** asset we created, we will see one node, the **ROOT**:

From this node, we can start to make decisions about how this AI will behave. For now, just to see how everything is set up, let's make our AI play an animation and then wait a few seconds before repeating this loop:

1. From the dark box at the bottom of the **ROOT** node, drag a connection off and create a **Sequence** node.
2. From the bottom of the **Sequence** node, drag a connection off toward the left and create a **Play Animation** node.
3. With the **Play Animation** node selected, go into the **Content Browser** and into the Mannequin\Animations folder.
4. Select the **Equip_Rifle_Standing** animation.

5. Back in the Behavior Tree's **Play Animation** node, in the **Details** panel, press the left arrow next to the **Node | Animation to Play** property to apply the equip animation.

6. From the **Sequence** node again, drag another connection off toward the right and create a **Wait** node.

7. In this **Wait** node's properties, set the **Wait | Wait Time** to **2** seconds.

The Behavior Tree should look like this now:

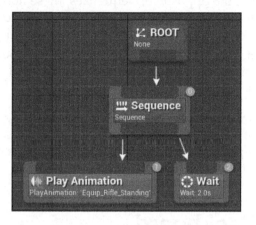

That's all we need to do for now, so save this Behavior Tree. Now, if we run the game, we'll see our character animate, then wait, then animate again in a loop. If we watch the Behavior Tree while the game is running we'll also see it highlighting which path it's using, which is an incredibly useful debugging tool:

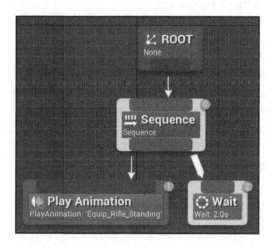

There are a few things to note about Behavior Trees. The **ROOT** node can only have one connection, and it must be a **Composite** node. Composite nodes can be any of the following:

- **Sequences**: These run their attached nodes from left to right. If one of its children fails (for instance, it has an attached condition that's not met), it will abort the sequence and go back to the **Sequences** parent node to figure out what to do next.
- **Selectors**: Almost the opposite of **Sequences**, these nodes will run their children from left to right until one of them *succeeds*. Once that child has finished executing, the **Selector** node passes the decision making back to its parent.
- **Simple Parallel**: This lets us run a single task alongside a more complex tree. These are not commonly used, since **Services** (covered later in this chapter) can provide more flexibility.

We'll see these processes in action in a bit, but, for now, our AI needs a little work. It's not even doing what we had it doing before, which was running to random locations. By default, there's no task for picking a random location, so we'll need to make one ourselves. The first step for this is setting up a Blackboard.

Setting up a Blackboard

Behavior Trees have no variables themselves, so they are stored in another asset called a Blackboard. The Behavior Tree can modify values on this Blackboard and then use them when making decisions or running tasks. In our case, we'll want a location that our AI will be moving to, so let's create the Blackboard:

1. In the **Content Browser**, go to the `ThirdPersonBP\Blueprints` folder.
2. Right-click, and under **Artificial Intelligence**, select Blackboard.
3. Name this new asset **EnemyBlackboard**.
4. Open up this new asset. Its interface is pretty simple. On the left, we'll have an empty list of keys, which is our main concern.
5. Press the **New Key** button, then scroll down and select **Vector** as the type for this **New Key**.
6. Name this **New Key** `TargetLocation`.

Our Blackboard should now have the following:

That's all we need to do here, so save the Blackboard asset.

Assigning the Blackboard to a Behavior Tree

Now, we need to assign this Blackboard to our Behavior Tree. This is simple:

1. Open our **EnemyBehavior** Behavior Tree asset.
2. With no node selected, go into the **Details** tab on the right.
3. Under the **AI | Behavior Tree | Blackboard Asset** property, click the drop-down box and select our **EnemyBlackboard** asset.

Now, the Blackboard is assigned to this Behavior Tree, and we can access the **TargetLocation** value. The next step we need to do is create our own task to assign a value to that Blackboard value.

Creating a Behavior Tree task

Tasks are created as separate Blueprint assets, and, by default, will be created in the same folder as the Behavior Tree. The easiest way to create them is directly from the Behavior Tree, so let's do that now:

1. At the top of our **EnemyBehavior** window, click on the **New Task** button. This will create the asset and open it up for us.
2. The names given to new tasks by default are not useful, so let's go into the **ThirdPersonBP\Blueprints** folder and find the **Task**. (The icon will be a hollow circle, and its name will start with BTTask_BlueprintBase_New.) Rename it BT_GetRandomLocation.

Back in the task's Blueprint, instead of using an **Event**, such as **BeginPlay**, Tasks have their own set of events:

The most common one is **Receive Execute AI**, which is called each time the Behavior Tree branches onto this task. This event has **Owner Controller** and **Controlled Pawn** as outputs, giving us easy access to those.

Since Behavior Trees are not limited to enemies, non-player characters (NPCs), or even Pawns/Controllers, there is an alternate **Receive Execute** event that has the **Owner Actor** as its output.

Two other **Events** available to us are common in latent tasks (such as the **Wait** node we used), **Receive Tick** and **Receive Tick AI**, which have **Delta Seconds** available as well as the previously mentioned, **Owner Actor** or **Owner Controller/Controlled Pawn**.

For our custom task, we'll be using **Receive Execute AI**, since we want easy access to the **Controlled Pawn** to get its location. Let's set up our script:

1. Create the **Receive Execute AI** node.
2. From the **Controlled Pawn** output, create a **Get Actor Location** node.
3. From this node, create a **Get Random Point In Navigable Radius** node.
4. We may want to change the **Radius** we use in different circumstances, so create a **Float** variable in this class and name it Radius. Connect this **Radius** variable to the **Radius** input of the **Get Random Point** node. Luckily, creating variables here lets us set them directly in the Behavior Tree, so we won't need to create a duplicate task for a different radius or change this value through code.
5. Set the **Radius** variable to **Instance Editable** so it can be set back in the Behavior Tree.
6. Now that we have our random location, we need to set our Blackboard value with it. This isn't done directly, since tasks can be generalized and made extremely flexible. Instead, we pass the value to a **Key**. From the execution output of the **Receive Execute AI** node, create a **Set Blackboard Value as Vector** node.

7. Connect the **Random Location** output of the **Get Random Point** node to the **Value** input of the **Set Blackboard Value** node.

8. Now for the **Key**. Create a new variable, and set its type to `Blackboard Key Selector`. Name it `LocationKey`, and set it to **Instance Editable**.

9. Connect this variable to the **Key** input of the **Set Blackboard Value** node.

10. Now, we need to let the Behavior Tree know that this task is done. From the **Set Blackboard Value** node, create a **Finish Execute** node.

11. Connect the **Return Value** of the **Get Random Point** node to the **Success** input of the **Finish Execute** node. This will let the Behavior Tree know whether this task failed or not.

The code in this task should now look like this:

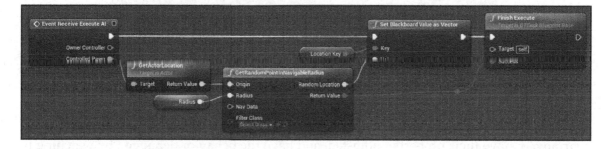

We've completed this custom task, so compile, save, and close this file.

Now, we can set up our Behavior Tree to mimic the code we had at the beginning of the chapter:

1. Open our `EnemyBehavior` file.

2. Delete the **Play Animation** node.

3. Create one of our custom **Get Random Location** nodes and attach it to the **Sequence**.

4. Select the new node, and, in the **Details** tab on the right, set the **Radius** to **2000** and the **Location Key** to **TargetLocation**.

5. In between the **Get Random Location** node and the **Wait** node, create a **Move To** node and connect it to the **Sequence**.

6. In the **Move To** node's properties, set its **Blackboard | Blackboard Key** to **TargetLocation**.

The Behavior Tree should look like this:

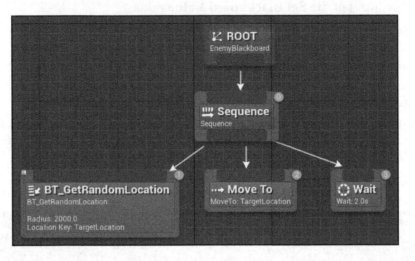

We will now save our Behavior Tree file and run the game. We'll now be able to see our AI moving to random locations again!

Compare this Behavior Tree to the code we created at the beginning of the chapter. We can easily see how much more flexible a Behavior Tree can be. These nodes can easily be rearranged, have their properties adjusted, and have the behavior debugged by watching it in action. With more complex AI, having all of this in code can quickly become overwhelming and difficult to debug compared to a Behavior Tree.

Now that we have a simple AI working with a Behavior Tree, let's add a bit more to it. We'll have the AI stop and face us if we get too close. We haven't given him a gun or even an equip animation, so the most he can do is stare at us menacingly.

To do this we'll need to work with a Selector.

Selectors

Right now, we're only using a **Sequence** in our Behavior Tree, but, in order to interrupt its loop, we'll need to use a **Selector**. Remember that a **Selector** will run its children until one of them succeeds; so, if we put this new set of *stare at the player* nodes to the left of our run to *random locations* sequence, it will run that sequence if the right conditions are met.

First, we need to set up the composite nodes:

1. Move the *run to random locations* set of nodes down and to the right.
2. From the **ROOT** node, create a **Selector** node.
3. Connect this **Selector** node to the **Sequence** node.
4. Now we'll create the **Branch**. From the **Selector** node, create another **Sequence** node to the left of the first one.
5. Under this new **Sequence** node, create a **Wait** node.

The Behavior Tree should now look like this:

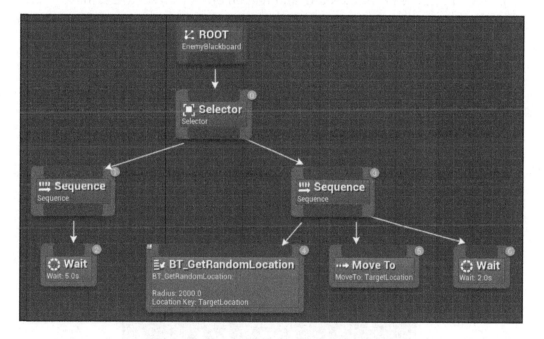

If we run the game now, the AI won't do anything. If we look in the Behavior Tree while it's running, we'll see that the **Wait** node to the far left is the only node that's being executed. This is because the **Selector** is checking its children from left to right until it finds one that succeeds, then, after that child is done executing, the **Selector** passes the decision making back up to its parent. The second **Sequence** can never execute, because the first one will never fail. Let's change this by adding a **Decorator**.

Decorators

Decorators can be added to composite nodes (selectors, sequences, and simple parallels) in order to give them a pass/fail condition. If we add a **Decorator** to the **Sequence** node on the left, if the **Decorator** fails, the **Selector** will try to run the **Sequence** on the right instead.

Let's set up our Blackboard and Behavior Tree to see this in action:

1. Open our `EnemyBlackboard` file.
2. Add a new **Vector Key** and name it **SeenPlayerLocation**.
3. Save and close the Blackboard, and reopen our `EnemyBehavior` file.
4. On the left **Sequence**, right-click and select **Add Decorator | Blackboard**. This will check whether a **Blackboard** value is **set**. If not, it will fail.
5. Click on the **Decorator** to select it, and, in the **Details** tab on the right, set its **Blackboard Key** to **SeenPlayerLocation**.

The left-hand side of the Behavior Tree should look like this now:

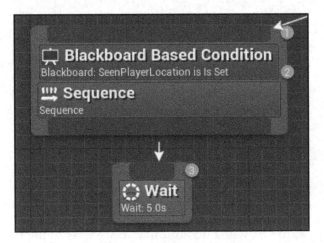

Save the Behavior Tree and run the game. We'll see that now the left **Sequence** never executes, because we'll never set this new **SeenPlayerLocation** key. So, it will run our **move to random locations** sequence in a loop. All good, so far.

Now, we need a way to set this **SeenPlayerLocation** key. To do that, we'll use a **Service**.

Services

Services, like **Decorators**, are attached to **Composite** nodes. Services run at a predetermined interval as long as the **Composite** node they're attached to is being run. We'll use a **Service** to check for the player's location, and set the **SeenPlayerLocation** key if the player is close enough to this enemy:

1. Click the **New Service** button at the top of our Behavior Tree.
2. In the `ThirdPersonBP\Blueprints` folder in the **Content Browser**, locate this new asset (its name will start with `BTService_BlueprintBase_New`), and rename it `BTS_CheckSeePlayer`.
3. Now, we need to add the code that will detect the player.
4. In this new asset's Blueprint window, create a **Receive Tick AI** event. Unlike normal ticks, this event is run at an interval that we specify when we add this **Service** to our Behavior Tree. Because of this, we can run code that could normally impact performance too much if run every frame.
5. From the **Receive Tick AI** node, create a **Get All Actors of Class** node and set its **Actor** class to **ThirdPersonCharacter**. This will search for our player.
6. From this **Get All Actors** node, create a **ForEach** loop from the **Out Actors** array.
7. From the **Array Element** output of the **ForEach** loop, create a **Get Actor Location** node.
8. Back at the beginning, create a **Get Actor Location** from the controlled Pawn output of the **Receive Tick AI** event as well.

So far, our code should look like this:

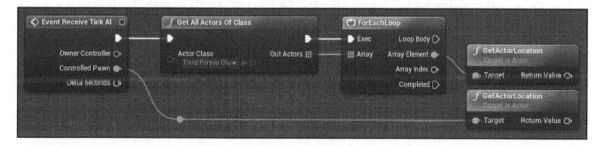

9. From the **Get Actor Location** outputs, create a **Vector - Vector** node and connect both of them.
10. From the output of this node, create a **Vector Length** node.
11. From the **Vector Length** node, create a **Float < Float** node.

12. We'll want to adjust the detection radius for the player, so let's create a **Float** variable named `DetectionRadius`. Make sure that it's set to **Instance Editable**.

13. Connect this **DetectionRadius** variable to the bottom input of the **Float < Float** node.

This section of the code should look like this:

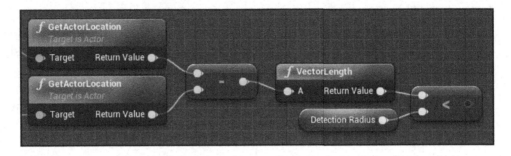

14. From the output of the **Float < Float** node, create a **Branch**.

15. Connect the **Loop Body** output of the **ForEachLoop** to the **Branch**.

16. Now ,we need a Blackboard **Key**. Create a new variable named `LocationKey` and set its type to **Blackboard Key Selector**. Make sure that **Instance Editable** is checked.

17. From the **True** output of the **Branch** node, create a **Set Blackboard Value as Vector** node.

18. Connect our **LocationKey** variable to the **Key** input of this **Set Blackboard Value** node.

19. For the **Value** input, connect the top Get Actor Location node to it (the one coming off of the **ForEachLoop**). This will set the Blackboard value to the player's location.

20. There's one final step. From the **False** output of the **Branch**, create a **Clear Blackboard Value** node. This will make sure the **Decorator** we set up earlier fails if the player is too far away.

21. Connect the **Location Key** variable to the **Clear Blackboard Value** node.

This final section of code should look like this:

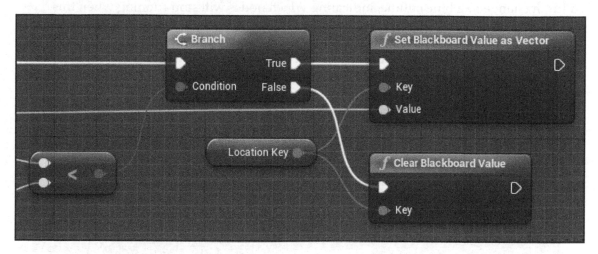

Compile, save, and close this file.

Setting up Service in Blackboard

Back in the Blackboard, we can now set up this **Service**:

1. Open the `EnemyBehavior` file.
2. In the **Selector** node, right-click and select **Add Service | BTS Check See Player**.
3. Click on this **Service** to select it, and, in its properties, set **Detection Radius** to **500** and **Location Key** to **SeenPlayerLocation**. We will also set its **Interval** to **0.2** and its **Random Deviation** to **0.0**. These are the time values I was referring to when I was discussing how frequently the **Tick** event in our **Service** will run.
4. Delete the **Wait** node below the left **Sequence**.
5. From the left **Sequence**, create a **Rotate To Face BBEntry** task.
6. In this **Task's** properties, set its **Blackboard Key** to **SeenPlayerLocation**.
7. There's one final step. The **Decorator** in the left **Sequence** has a property that needs to be changed. Click on **Blackboard Based Condition** in our left **Sequence** and look at its properties. We'll see a **Flow Control** section that has a property called **Observer Aborts**. This property determines what happens when its Blackboard Key's value changes. In our case, we want the AI to stop immediately and face the player, so we'll set **Observer Aborts** to **Lower Priority**.

When we change that **Observer Aborts** property, we'll see the right **Sequence** and all of its children change to a blue outline, indicating which nodes will stop running when this **Blackboard Based Condition**'s value changes. This will make the **Selector** reevaluate which of its children to run. When **SeenPlayerLocation** is set, it will run the left **Sequence** node, and with **SeenPlayerLocation** cleared, it will run the right **Sequence**.

Our Behavior Tree should now look like this:

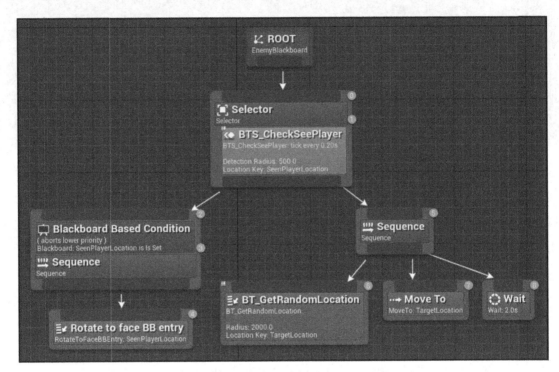

Save the Behavior Tree and run the game while keeping an eye on the Behavior Tree. We'll see that, when we get close to the AI, it will stop executing the right **Sequence** and start using the left one, which makes it stop and stare at us menacingly:

I think he's saying *you're lucky you didn't give me a gun.*

Summary

In this chapter, we've learned how to create some simple AI by making our own Pawn and Controller with some code to make them run around a Nav Mesh. Then, we expanded on this by creating our own Behavior Tree with tasks, decorators, and services to expand on our AI's behavior.

You can see how Behavior Trees make creating complex AI a lot simpler. If we tried to do even this simple one in code, it would quickly become a complicated mess. It would be difficult to make major modifications, and it would be difficult to debug.

Even the code we made that detects the player can be simplified and made a lot more flexible. For more advanced reading, look into adding an AI perception component to the enemy's controller class: https://docs.unrealengine.com/en-us/Engine/Components/AI.

In the next chapter, we'll take a look at creating multiplayer games, and the features of Blueprint that will help us keep everything in sync. Onward!

Multiplayer Games

7

In this chapter, we're going to talk about multiplayer games, the different design and thought processes that go into them, and the Blueprint code that goes into making one. By the end of this chapter, we should have a good idea of how to go about creating a multiplayer game without getting caught in some of the common pitfalls.

When deciding to create a multiplayer game, it's important to start the framework for your game with multiplayer in mind from the beginning. It can be extremely difficult to add multiplayer to a game that wasn't created with it in mind. In some cases, vast portions of code must be entirely rewritten to get a game working in multiplayer.

The following topics will be covered in this chapter:

- The client-server model
- Replication
- Multiplayer classes

Let's take a look at how a multiplayer game works.

The client–server model

Unreal Engine 4 works on what's called the client-server model, where the server is the ultimate authority. This means that the server controls the state of the game and gives any relevant information to each connected client. If you've ever experienced lag where you seem to teleport, this is you as the client predicting where you are, and the server saying *no, you're over here*.

The client-server model works well when it minimizes the amount of information being transmitted over the network, so optimization of your network code is important. Luckily for us, the Unreal Engine has many built-in tools and functionality to help us with that.

Let's see how this can help us with Awesome Game.

Testing a listen server

For this quick start guide, we'll be testing multiplayer using a listen server instead of a dedicated server. Dedicated server functionality is not something that the Unreal Engine provides out of the box and will require you to download and compile the Unreal Engine source code yourself in order to set it up. More information about that process is on the wiki: `https://wiki.unrealengine.com/Dedicated_Server_Guide_(Windows_%26_Linux)`.

For Awesome Game, we will just use a listen server. The difference from a dedicated server is that the server is also a client and is called the host.

The thought process and coding practices for dedicated and listen servers are mostly the same, however, with only a few tiny differences that we will discuss in this chapter.

Testing a listen server from the editor is simple. In the main editor window, if we click the down arrow next to the **Play** button to open up the **Play** options, we'll see two settings that we can change:

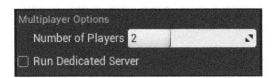

Setting the **Number of Players** to anything but 1 will run the editor windows in a client-server environment. And although there is a **Run Dedicated Server** option listed, keep in mind that this is **ONLY** for in-editor testing and won't be available in a packaged project unless you follow the guide in the wiki I listed earlier to compile the engine yourself.

For now, we'll set the **Number of Players** to 2 and keep the **Run Dedicated Server** box unchecked. Now, when we hit **Play**, two windows will appear instead of one:

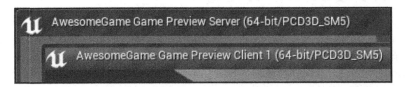

We will be able to tell them apart by reading the window's header. In this case, we have **Server** and **Client 1** windows. This can be useful when debugging to figure out where the bug is occurring. Knowing whether it is only happening on the client, only on the server, or on both can help to narrow it down.

Now, with both windows running, let's play a game of spot the difference. If we try different things such as running into our pickup spheres or equipping our weapon, we will see that the game does not act the same on the server and client (use *Alt + Tab* to switch between the two running game windows):

Here, the pickup sphere, player material change, and weapon equip has happened on one window but not the other. This highlights the need to keep multiplayer in mind when designing your game. Awesome Game isn't quite an awesome multiplayer game, but we can fix that. And we will.

Let's talk about replication.

Replication

Replication is the process by which games transmit data over the network to keep clients in sync with the server. For the Unreal Engine, we can see that a lot of the work is already done for us. The player location, movement, and jumping is replicated in the third-person template we've been using. However, anything we add to our project must be replicated properly to prevent bugs like this from occurring.

Not everything needs to be replicated, though. The server doesn't care if you're in your game's settings menu adjusting the resolution or key binds, and the other clients certainly don't need to know. Knowing *what* to replicate is actually more important than knowing *how* to replicate, since you run the risk of lag and other network problems if you *overshare*, so to speak.

There are also ways to fake things to further improve performance. Take the case of firing a weapon. The server definitely needs to know exactly where you are and where you're looking when you fire so it can check whether you hit anything. For other clients, most of this is not important. The server can simply tell them *this player fired their gun* so those clients can create the necessary sound and particle effects. Those clients already know approximately where the firing player is and where they're facing, even though it may not be precise down to the decimals due to the latency. Sending the exact location and rotation is an unnecessary use of bandwidth, especially since the server will notify everyone if something was hit.

Now that we have some idea of the best use of replication, let's take a look at some specifics while fixing Awesome Game. We'll start with variables.

Variable replication

Variables are the simplest form of replication. When a variable changes, we may or may not need to tell the clients about it.

Let's take a game with an inventory system as an example. Depending on our game design, we may or may not want to let other players know when someone is browsing their inventory so we can play a special animation. That could be done with an `IsBrowsingInventory` Boolean.

For Awesome Game, one of our problems can be fixed quite simply by using variable replication. Let's take a look at our player material problem.

If we take a look at our `Pickup_MaterialSwitcher` class `HandlePickedUp` event, we can see that it applies its material to the mesh of the player that picked it up. This works fine in single player mode, but for multiplayer we need to let everyone know about this change. To do this, we can use a variable for the material. Let's set that up and take a look at the replication properties:

1. Open the `ThirdPersonCharacter` Blueprint.
2. Create a new variable and name it `PickupMaterial`. Set its type to **Material Interface**.
3. Compile and save the `ThirdPersonCharacter` Blueprint.
4. Open the `Pickup_MaterialSwitcher` Blueprint.
5. Go to the **Handle Picked Up** event in the **Event Graph**.

6. Delete the **Target | Mesh** node connected to the event, and the **Set Material** node it's connected to as well.
7. From the event's **Picked Up By** output, create a **SET** node for the PickupMaterial variable we created.
8. Connect the **Get Material** node's output to the **SET** node's PickupMaterial input.
9. Connect the event's output to this new node, and the new node's output to the **Parent** function call.

The new event code should look like this:

Compile, save, and close this Blueprint.

Now we have the variable being set, so let's take a look at replicating it. If we open up our **ThirdPersonCharacter** Blueprint again and click on the PickupMaterial variable, we can see, in the **Details** tab, an option near the bottom of the **Variable** category called **Replication**, with three options in the drop-down box:

By default, variables are set to **None**, so no replication will occur.

The second option is **Replicated**. When a variable's value changes, the new value will be sent to all clients. This might seem like the option we need, but nothing actually happens when this value is sent to the clients. If this were something we were checking every frame, for instance, a health value that's displayed as a bar above other players, setting a variable to **Replicated** would be all we need. But checking our `PickupMaterial` variable every frame would be horribly unoptimized, so there's a third option for variable replication: **RepNotify**.

RepNotify calls a function when a variable change is sent over the network. If we set our `PickupMaterial` variable to **RepNotify**, we'll see a new function added to our class, **OnRep_PickupMaterial**:

RepNotify functions are a convenient way to deal with the variable change only when it actually changes. In our case, we want to apply the new material to the player when `PickupMaterial` changes, so let's add that to this new function:

1. Set the `PickupMaterial` variable to `RepNotify` if you haven't already done so.
2. Double-click the `OnRep_PickupMaterial` function to open it up.
3. Drag a reference to our **Mesh** component from the top-left tab onto the **Graph**.
4. From the **Mesh** variable's output, create a **Set Material** node.
5. Drag a reference to our `PickupMaterial` function onto the graph and connect it to the **Set Material's** Material input. We'll notice that it has an icon with two spheres in the upper right-hand corner, letting us know that this is a replicated variable.

The function should look like this:

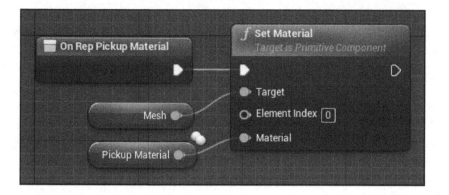

Compile and save this Blueprint.

Now, when we run the game and pick up one of the spheres, we'll see the material change on both the client and the server. That's one problem down!

Next, we'll solve our other two bugs using replication for events.

Event replication

In addition to passing variable values, event calls can also be replicated. As we discussed in Chapter 2, *Programming Using Blueprints*, this only applies to events, not functions, so that's one thing to keep in mind when making the decision to use an event or a function for a block of code.

One major difference between variable and event replication is that event replication can go in either direction. The server has to know when we've equipped our weapon and when we've fired it, for instance. This is done through event replication and will help us to fix our weapon equipping issue.

Let's fix that bug now. Open up the **ThirdPersonCharacter** Blueprint and find our **InputAction Equip** event. The code here will have to be divided into three separate blocks of code to work correctly through replication. Here is the break down:

- The client tells the server they would like to equip/unequip their weapon.
- The server changes the WeaponEquipped variable and replicates it to all clients.
- The clients show/hide the weapon and alter their animation state based on this new WeaponEquipped value.

Let's tackle this one step at a time. First, let's tell the server we want to change our equip status:

1. Right-click on the **InputAction Equip** node's output and select **Break Link** to disconnect the rest of the code. Move this code below the event.
2. Below the **Equip** event, right-click and create a **Custom Event**. Name it `ServerEquip`.
3. Connect the `ServerEquip` event's output to the **SET** node we disconnected in step **1**.
4. Delete the **NOT**, **My Weapon**, and **Set Actor Hidden** nodes at the end of this block of code.
5. From the **InputAction Equip** node's **Pressed** output, create a call to our **ServerEquip** event.

The code should look like this now:

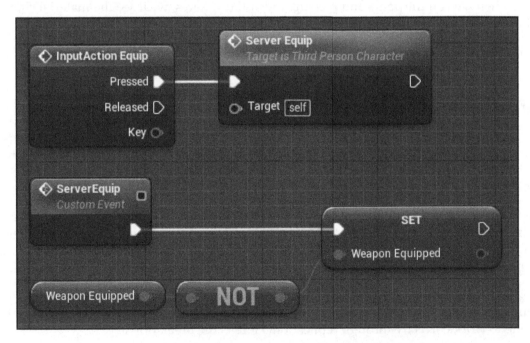

We will be coming back to this **ServerEquip** event in a second, but first let's take care of the variable replication:

1. Select the `bWeaponEquipped` variable in the **My Blueprint** tab on the left-hand side.
2. In the **Details** tab on the right, set the `bWeaponEquipped` variable's **Replication** property to `RepNotify`. This will create an `OnRep_bWeaponEquipped` function.
3. Open the `OnRep_bWeaponEquipped` function.
4. Drag a reference to our `MyWeapon` variable out onto this function.
5. From its output, create a **Set Actor Hidden In Game** node.
6. Connect the execution output of the function to the input of this **Set Actor Hidden** node.
7. Drag a reference to the `bWeaponEquipped` variable onto the graph.
8. From its output, create a **NOT** node.
9. Connect the **NOT** node to the **New Hidden** input of the **Set Actor Hidden** node.

The code should look like this now:

We're almost done, but the **ServerEquip** event call is not being replicated. Let's go back to the **Event Graph**. Click on the **ServerEquip** event and take a look at the **Details** tab. We'll see two replication properties that will interest us:

The first property is a drop-down list determining who runs this function. The choices are as follows:

- **Not Replicated**: The default for Events. This can be called from any other code running on the server or client, but the event call will not be replicated.
- **Multicast**: Calling this event will cause it to be called on the server and all clients, but ONLY if this is called from the server. Calling this from a client will only run the code on that client.
- **Run on Server**: When this is called from a client, the event call will be replicated to the server. The code attached will ONLY run on the server and will not even run on the client that called it.
- **Run on owning Client**: Sometimes, we will want code to run on a client, but *only* on the client that owns the object it's being called on, in this case, a Pawn. Let's say a player wants to interact with an object, and we want that object to tell the player which menu Blueprint to open. We could call an event with the menu class as a parameter, but the other clients don't care about this event call and shouldn't run the code. In a case like that, we would set the event to **Run on owning Client** so it doesn't get called for everybody.

In our case, we want to tell the server to change our equip status, so let's set the **ServerEquip** event to **Run on Server**.

The second property, below this drop-down box, is a **Reliable** checkbox. This determines whether the event absolutely must be called and will repeat the call in cases of packet loss or heavy network load until it is called successfully.

This is used as an optimization technique. A majority of events we will want to be **Reliable**, since there's nothing more frustrating to a player than clicking a button and having nothing happen. Sometimes, however, the event call doesn't matter that much. Let's say we have an event that spawns a particle effect and sound effect on players that level up, so other players can see it happen. In the grand scheme of things, it's not incredibly important that other players see that, and we can leave that event's Reliable checkbox unchecked so that, in cases of heavy network load, it can focus on more important things.

For our **ServerEquip** event, we definitely want the server to run it, so let's check the Reliable box.

Now, if we compile the `ThirdPersonCharacter` class and run the game, we can see the weapon being equipped on both screens:

Ok, that's two problems down! Next, we'll take a look at flow control to ensure code runs only where we want it to.

Flow control in multiplayer

Sometimes, we'll want to *prevent* an event from running on either the server or the client. For an example of this, let's make a quick modification to our `BasePickup` class:

1. Open the **BasePickup** Blueprint.
2. In the **Event Graph's On Component Begin Overlap** event, right-click on the output execution pin and **Other Actor** output pin and select **Break Link** to disconnect the rest of the code. Don't delete the **Cast** or **Handle Picked Up** nodes, just move them to the side for now.
3. From the **On Component Begin Overlap** node, create a **Print String** node, and set its **In String** to something like **BasePickup collided!**.
4. Compile and save this Blueprint.

Now, when we run the game and pick up one of the spheres, we'll see two messages on the screen:

We'll see that the message has logged for both the server and the client. To be clear, this is not what we want. Remember that the server is the authority when it comes to the game's state. The client should not be determining whether a pickup was picked up or not. That's the server's job.

The only problem with this is that, if we select the **On Component Begin Overlap** event, we won't see any properties in the **Details** tab, so there's no way to actually prevent this event from running on clients. There is, however, a way to keep the rest of the code and the **Handle Picked Up** function from being called. To do this, we'll need to know whether this code is running on the server or client. Luckily, there is a built-in node available that lets us know. Let's add it now:

1. Open the **BasePickup** Blueprint.
2. Delete the **Print String** node.
3. Right-click next to the **On Component Begin Overlap** node and create an **Is Server** node.
4. From the **Is Server** node's output, create a **Branch** node.
5. From the **True** output of the **Branch** node, connect to the **Cast** node that we moved aside earlier.
6. Reconnect the **Other Actor** output of the event to the **Object** input of the **Cast** node.

The code should now look like this:

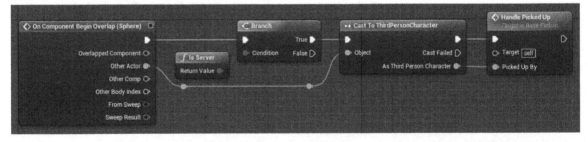

Compile and save this Blueprint. Now we've ensured that the **Handle Picked Up** function is only called by the server. We can test this by adding a **Print String** node inside the **Handle Picked Up** function, like this:

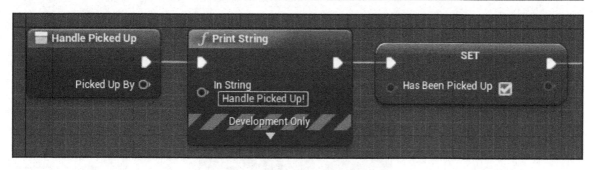

If we compile that and run it, no matter who picks up a sphere, that **Print String** message will only show as running on the server.

The **Is Server** node is also a useful tool when you only want certain sections of code to run on a server or client. Sometimes, even functions that need to run on both will have sections that you only want to run on one or the other.

For example, let's say we had a **kick player** option in our **Pause** menu. We would only want to show that on the server, so, in the pause menu's Construct function, we could check the **Is Server** node and hide that section of the menu, while letting other construct code run on both.

So, now we have the **Handle Picked Up** function only running on the server, and that function destroys the pickup, but the pickup remains on the client. What's going on here? To figure this one out, we're going to have to look at actor replication.

Actor replication

In addition to variables and events, actors themselves can be replicated. It may seem like we'd want ALL actors to be replicated, for example, we would want projectiles fired from a gun to show on the server and all clients. However, sometimes this isn't the case. Let's say we had a racing game that had huge arrows showing each player where to turn. The code for those would run client-side, and indeed, the server might not need to know about them at all. In cases like that, we could leave the actor's replication turned off to save bandwidth.

In our pickup's case, however, the lack of replication is causing it to not disappear on the client when picked up. The reason for this is that, when an actor in a level is not replicated, it exists on both the server and the client, but they're not technically the same object. When the Destroy function is called when it's picked up, the server thinks the object only exists on the server and doesn't know that it also exists on the clients.

Fixing this is simple and will also give us a chance to look at some other properties useful for actor replication. If we open our **BasePickup Blueprint** and click the **Class Defaults** button at the top, we can see some useful variables in the **Replication** section of the **Details** panel:

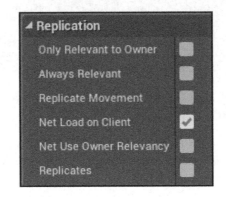

Let's take a look at what these do:

- **Only Relevant to Owner**: Much like the **Run on Owning Client** event replication option, this property is useful if the entire actor only needs to exist on the owning client. As an example of this, first-person shooters often use separate objects to represent weapons in first-person view and show them in another player's hands in third-person. The first-person weapon would only need to exist on the owning client.
- **Always Relevant**: This actor should always be relevant, even when the client can't see it or it is on the other side of the world. This one should be used sparingly, since replicating things the player can't see can eat up bandwidth.
- **Replicate Movement**: Leave this unchecked if the actor is stationary, otherwise check it so the position will be updated.
- **Net Load on Client**: If this is unchecked, the level-placed object will not be loaded on clients, only on the server.
- **Net Use Owner Relevancy**: If this object is owned by a player, it will use that player's relevancy to determine the object's (if the player object is **Always Relevant** this will be too, for example).
- **Replicates**: This determines whether this class replicates at all. Leave this unchecked for non-gameplay objects that don't need to be synchronized.

For our pickup, the only thing we need to change is checking the Replicates property. Once we do that and compile the Blueprint, we will see the pickup disappear properly on the client when either the server or the client picks it up.

And with that, all of the multiplayer bugs with Awesome Game are fixed.

There are only a few more things we need to talk about as far as multiplayer is concerned, starting with the overall structure of Unreal Engine 4's multiplayer-specific classes.

Multiplayer classes

Unreal Engine's class structure is set up to take advantage of multiplayer and do a lot of the heavy lifting for us. Instead of reinventing this structure, we can use it to make multiplayer development a lot easier. But to do this, we need to know what's available for us to use.

Let's take a look at the classes that are specific to multiplayer.

GameMode and GameState

Although GameMode exists in single player mode as well, it is set up with multiplayer in mind. Its purpose is to control everything about the game that's not specific to the players themselves. Handling players connecting and disconnecting, choosing spawn locations, determining the Pawn class that a player uses: those are all functions of GameMode.

It's important to note that GameMode does not exist on clients and attempts to access it will return a null reference.

There are a lot of things the player will want to have access to that should be under the control of the GameMode class, such as team scores and other non-player specific variables. For these, we have GameState. This is a replicated class that can be used to store such things as the remaining match time and whether or not team kills are enabled: so that we can have anything that we want the clients to know about displayed somewhere, for example.

These can be accessed from most other Blueprints with their **Get** nodes:

Keep in mind that these only return the base classes, so you will want to use a **Cast** node when working with your custom classes.

As we discussed in Chapter 2, *Programming Using Blueprints*, custom GameMode classes can be used by going into **Edit | Project Settings | Maps & Modes** and setting the **Default GameMode** there.

For GameStates, the property can be changed in the default properties of your custom **GameMode** (click on the **Class Defaults** in the top toolbar while editing your GameMode class).

> You may have noticed that the HUD is blank on the client. If we check the MyWidget class Update Remaining Spheres function, we'll see that we access GameMode. Since that doesn't exist on the client, the rest of the function will not run and the client's HUD will not update. Knowing what we know about GameState and RepNotify, see if you can move the Remaining Pickups variable to a custom GameState class and get the client's HUD updating.

Next, we have classes that are specific to players.

PlayerState, PlayerController, and Pawn

One very important thing to remember when working with player-specific replication is that PlayerController only exists on the server and the client that owns that PlayerController. Each client's PlayerController does not exist on any other client.

For abstract variables that don't apply to Pawns themselves (such as our WeaponEquipped variable), we have the PlayerState actor that we can use. Here, we can store things like that player's score, their stats if we want to share those with other players, or their name (which is already a PlayerState variable available to us).

PlayerStates can be accessed through either the Pawn or PlayerController class through a simple **Get** node for it:

Pawns should be used to store variables specific to the physical representation of the player. Things like the equipped weapon class, health, or what hat that player is wearing would be stored in the Pawn class.

All three of these classes can be customized and specified in the class defaults of your GameMode class.

Summary

Now that we've learned the specifics of replication and the default classes that are available to us, we can see how important it is to design with multiplayer in mind from the start rather than trying to implement it later. Even our simple Awesome Game pickups and weapon equipping needed significant changes to work in multiplayer. It's important to test frequently on both the server and client to make sure your code is functioning properly.

By default, the Unreal Engine is able to use Steam for multiplayer, but setting it up and connecting through your friends list requires a bit of extra setup. The documentation for a Steam setup is here: https://docs.unrealengine.com/en-US/Programming/Online/Steam.

And to connect to a multiplayer game through your Friends list, along with a host of other session functionality, I highly recommend Morden Tral's amazing advanced sessions plugin, available for free here: https://forums.unrealengine.com/community/community-content-tools-and-tutorials/41043-advanced-sessions-plugin.

And that's it for multiplayer. In the final chapter, we'll take a look at some techniques we can use to test and optimize our game, then package it up for distribution. We're almost there!

8
Optimization, Testing, and Packaging

We've come to the end of this book and the end of Awesome Game. We've put together some awesome Blueprints, worked with Animation Blueprints, got our AI to work with behavior trees, and even got our game functioning perfectly online.

It's about time we wrapped this project up, but we're not quite done yet. We might have some performance issues that we're worried about, and while the assets we've put together are pretty slick, we need to put the game into an .exe file for our players.

To that end, we need to talk about optimization, testing, and packaging. To start, let's take a look at how we can get our game to run better through some of the optimization tools UE4 provides.

The following topics will be covered in this chapter:

- Optimization
- The Profiler
- Blueprint nativization
- Debugging in UE4

Let's start by talking about a few ways that we can optimize our game.

Optimization

Although there are several tools available that we can use to figure out where our performance issues lie, it is still up to us to fix or change the code. Some of that comes down to proper programming techniques. A few things we can do to make sure our game's frame rate doesn't suffer are as follows:

- **Keep Tick code to a minimum**: Blueprint objects that use too much code in a Tick can have a devastating impact on performance, since Ticks run every frame. Gameplay code is mostly event-driven, so take advantage of that.
- **Let the engine do the heavy lifting**: If we have an object that needs to know if any players were within a certain distance, we could check those distances in a Tick or some quick timer, but this would be inefficient. Adding a sphere collision component to the Blueprint and using the **On Actor Begin Overlap** event would be much simpler and cleaner, and would run faster.
- **Get all the Actors of class nodes**: If you find yourself needing to use this in a Tick or another frequently run function, consider creating an array that you can store the values in and populate it in **Begin Play**, or have classes notified when a new instance is created or destroyed so that they can update their arrays when you know the contents will change.
- **Trace functions**: Traces let us figure out what object or objects are hit along a line. They can be expensive if run frequently, so using other conditions that may return false before running a trace (we only want to trace actors within a certain distance, so we check the distance first) will help avoid this problem.
- **Reorganize conditionals**: For `if` statements with multiple conditions, it's best to think about which conditions are more likely to return false and put those first to exit the statement as quickly as possible. Keep in mind that every condition attached to a single Branch node will be analyzed, so using multiple Branch nodes or creating a custom If node can help with optimization here.
- **Take advantage of bindings in UMG**: Even your UI can impact performance if it isn't optimized. Use bindings for properties wherever possible to avoid issues here, and avoid frequently grabbing variables from other objects that don't change often.

These are some great starting points for optimization, but we don't want to leave our performance issues up to guesswork. Even with all of these techniques implemented, we still need to know exactly where our performance issues are. For that, we can use the Profiler.

The Profiler

By using the Profiler, we can create a recording of the game's performance as it's running, and then take a look at the stats to see how long it's taking our code to run.

To test this, we're going to need to purposely make some terrible code:

1. Open the **ThirdPersonCharacter** Blueprint
2. In the **Event** Graph, create the **Tick** event
3. Create a **ForLoop** and connect it to the **Tick** event
4. In the **ForLoop**, set the **Last Index** to 10000
5. Create a new integer variable and name it TestInt
6. Create a **SET** variable for TestInt and connect it to the **Loop Body** and **Index** outputs of the **ForLoop**

The code should look like this:

This is some horribly unoptimized code—and is perfect for our needs. Let's create the profile for our game.

Under the **Play** button's drop-down menu, make sure that the **Number of Players** is set to 1 if it was still set to 2 for our multiplayer tests, and press **Play** to run the game. You'll notice that the game is stuttering heavily. Let's look at the FPS. Hit the tilde key (~) and type in stat fps:

Press *Enter*. The FPS counter will show on screen. As expected, our frame rate is terrible now:

Now, we can create a useful profile. To do this, we need to use two commands. To start the profile, we'll use the tilde key again and type in `stat startfile`, and, to stop it, we will type in `stat stopfile`. While the **Profiler** is running, we'll see some information in the top left corner:

Let it run for about 10 seconds to get a good profile. Once we type in `stat stopfile` to finish the profile, we can exit out of the game and go back to the editor. Now, we need a way to open the file we've created. To do that, open a folder and go to the location where you've installed the engine. We will need to open the frontend here:

```
UE_4.22\Engine\Binaries\Win64\UnrealFrontEnd.exe
```

Once the frontend is open, we'll need to go to the **Session FrontEnd** main tab and click on the **Profiler** tab:

Press the **Load** button and navigate to the AwesomeGame project folder. The profile will be here:

```
AwesomeGame\Saved\Profiling\UnrealStats
```

In this folder, you will find a UEDPIE folder with the map name, OS, and date and timestamp for when the profile was taken. In that folder is the actual .ue4stats profiles. Select the profile and open it up.

We will see a lot of information being displayed:

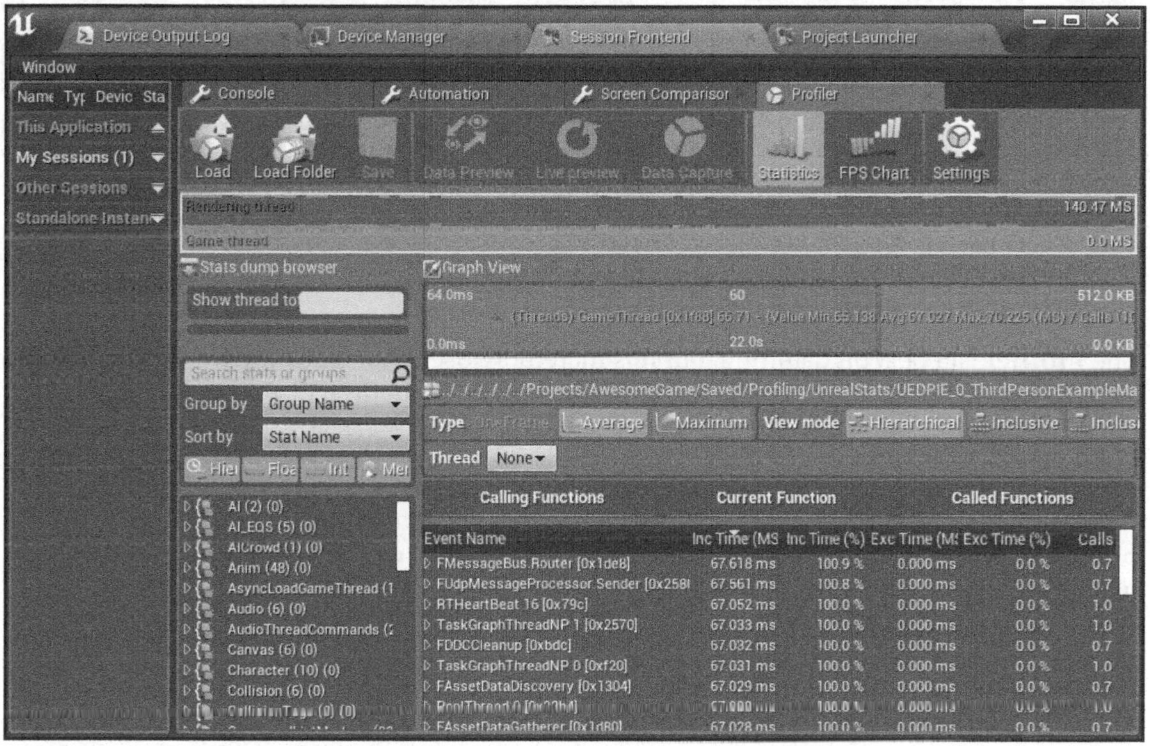

The main thing we are interested in here is the **Event Name** tab in the bottom right-hand corner. If we look at the **Inc Time** column (inclusive time, meaning it is the total time of that event and all of its children), we can see a lot of 60+ millisecond times. Our framerate issue is definitely in here somewhere.

For debugging Blueprints, we will want to scroll down until we find the **GameThread** event, and press the arrow to the left of it to dig down until we find the source of the framerate issue. We will eventually come across the **ThirdPersonCharacter ReceiveTick** event, as well as the **ExecuteUbergraph** section of it, which, in this instance, has an exclusive time of over 4,000 milliseconds:

This is definitely the source of the frame rate issue, and lines up perfectly with the code we added earlier.

Be sure to delete that code, by the way.

The **Profiler** can be a bit daunting, but it is incredibly useful for tracking down performance issues. For a more detailed look at what it can do, you will definitely want to read Epic's documentation for it: `https://docs.unrealengine.com/en-us/Engine/Performance/Profiler`.

If we've done everything we can and one or more of our Blueprints is still causing problems, we can convert the code into C++. Alternatively, we can let the engine do this for us with Blueprint Nativization.

Blueprint Nativization

Unreal Engine 4 has the ability to convert Blueprints into C++ code when packaging the game through Blueprint Nativization. It is disabled by default and unnecessary in most cases, but if you're trying to squeeze every bit of performance out of your project, you may consider doing this, if converting your code into C++ yourself isn't an option.

To enable Blueprint Nativization, go to **Edit** | **Project Settings**. In the **Project** | **Packaging** section, there will be a **Blueprints** section near the bottom. There are two options that we'll need to look at, as follows:

At the top, we have the Blueprint Nativization Method. By default this is disabled, but there are two other options:

- **Inclusive:** This will nativize all Blueprint assets
- **Exclusive**: This will only nativize Blueprint assets that are specified in the **List of Blueprint assets to nativize** option, below this option

For the most part, you will want to choose the Exclusive option, as this will keep the final executable from growing too large, and will keep unused Blueprints from being nativized.

Aside from optimization, we will also want to debug our game if our code isn't working properly. Let's take a look at that now.

Debugging in UE4

There's an old joke in programming that everyone just logs to the console to debug, and while print nodes in Blueprint and UE_Log statements in C++ are very useful for that, we should still know what other tools are available to us for debugging.

We've seen a bit of that with the behavior tree back in Chapter 6, *AI with the Behavior Tree and Blackboard*, where the tree highlighted which branches were currently running.

Regular Blueprints and animation Blueprints will also show what's currently being run. If we open the **ThirdPersonCharacter** Blueprint and go to the Event Graph's **InputAction Equip** node, when we run the game, we'll see the graph window outlined in orange with the word SIMULATING in the top right.

When we scroll the mouse wheel to toggle our weapon, we'll see the connecting line in the **InputAction** pulse red:

This can be a good way to follow what code is running if you're trying to figure out which parts of your code are not executing when you think they should be.

Blueprints can also have breakpoints, just like normal code can. If we right-click on a node and select **Toggle Breakpoint** (or select a node and use the *F9* shortcut), we can see that a breakpoint has been added to it. When we run the code and hit that breakpoint, the node will be highlighted with a red arrow. We can hover over variables to see their current value:

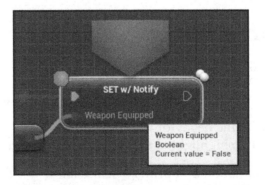

This is an incredibly useful tool for Blueprint debugging.

As far as C++ code is concerned, only one step is required to get breakpoints working. With both Visual Studio and the editor running, in Visual Studio, go to **Debug | Attach To Process**, and scroll down in the list until you find the UE4_Editor.exe process. Select that, and Visual Studio will now work properly with the breakpoints that you've set.

Now that our game is optimized and debugged, it's time for the final step.

Packing a project

This is it. It's time to package our game for distribution. Luckily, Unreal Engine does most of the work for us. The only thing we need to take care of is making sure we have our settings all sorted out for the build.

Let's take a look at the settings we need to adjust. Head into **Edit | Project Settings** and look at the sections under the **Project** category. There are five that we are interested in:

- **Description**: In this section, we set properties such as the **Project Name** and **Company Name**. There are also properties for **Licensing** and a **Privacy Policy** if desired.
- **Maps & Modes**: The two main properties that concern us here are the **Default Modes** and the **Game Default Map**. The **Game Default Map** is what will be loaded when the game starts, so this should be set to a main menu map or something similar.
- **Movies**: Any company logo startup movies can be added here and made skippable.
- **Packaging**: Here, you can switch between development and shipping builds by using the **Build Configuration** property. You may also want to check the **Full Rebuild** if major changes to your game have taken place between builds. A very important setting is under the advanced properties of the **Packaging** section (click the down arrow), which is the **List of Maps to Include** in a **Packaged Build**. All of the maps that you want in your packaged game should be specified here. This lets you exclude things like test maps.
- **Supported Platforms**: To save time and space, you should uncheck any platform that you will not be creating a build for.

Once all of your settings are adjusted, you can start a build by exiting the **Settings** menu and going to **File | Package Project**, and then selecting the desired platform. It will then ask you where you want the build to go. I recommend putting it somewhere outside of the project folder.

Once you select the location, the build will begin:

You can click the **Show Output Log** to follow along with the process. (This window can also be opened in **Window** | **Developer Tools** | **Output Log**.) If there are any problems, the errors will show up in red. If that happens, be sure to read the errors carefully to determine what happened, and search online for the error if you're not sure what it means.

Once the packaging is finished, you will get a completed message, and the log will let you know that **AutomationTool** has exited with **ExitCode 0** (success):

Congratulations! Go into the folder that you specified for the build, and you will see two folders and an executable:

AwesomeGame
Engine
AwesomeGame.exe

The executable and both folders will need to be distributed together in order for the game to function.

Summary

We've gone over quite a bit in this book, but there is a lot more to Unreal Engine than what was covered here. As you get comfortable with the editor and the process of making games, you will definitely want to expand your knowledge. There are a lot of resources available for you. A good starting point is Epic's documentation for the engine, which can be found at https://docs.unrealengine.com/en-us/, as well as the forums, where you can interact with the community, ask questions, and show off your work, at: https://forums.unrealengine.com/.

In addition, there are plenty of tutorials on YouTube and various blogs that cover every topic imaginable.

Have fun with Unreal Engine, and good luck with your project! Thank you for reading this book, and I sincerely hope it helped.

Another Book You May Enjoy

If you enjoyed this book, you may be interested in these other books by Packt:

Unreal Engine Blueprints Visual Scripting Projects
Lauren S. Ferro

ISBN: 978-1-78953-242-5

- Set up Unreal Engine and all of its foundational components
- Add basic movement to game objects and create collision mechanism
- Design and implement interfaces to extend player interaction
- Create a dynamically filling inventory system along with a UI to interact with it
- Add audio effects based on triggered events to various parts of the game environment
- Use analytic information to tune their game values
- Create complex enemy AI that can sense the world around it in a multiplayer game
- Deploy your game to multiple platforms and share it with the world

Leave a review - let other readers know what you think

Please share your thoughts on this book with others by leaving a review on the site that you bought it from. If you purchased the book from Amazon, please leave us an honest review on this book's Amazon page. This is vital so that other potential readers can see and use your unbiased opinion to make purchasing decisions, we can understand what our customers think about our products, and our authors can see your feedback on the title that they have worked with Packt to create. It will only take a few minutes of your time, but is valuable to other potential customers, our authors, and Packt. Thank you!

Index

C

D

E

F

G

H

I

Made in the USA
Coppell, TX
23 September 2020